Case Study Research Methods

Bill Gillham

continuum
LONDON • NEW YORK

Continuum
The Tower Building
11 York Road
London SE1 7NX
www.continuumbooks.com

370 Lexington Avenue
New York
NY 10017–6503

First published 2000

Reprinted 2001

British Library Cataloguing-in-Publication Data
A catalogue record for this book is available from the British Librar

ISBN 0 8264 4796 1

Typeset by Paston PrePress Ltd, Beccles, Suffolk
Printed and bound in Great Britain by TJ International Ltd.,
Padstow, Cornwall.

Contents

Series Foreword

The books in this series are intended for those doing small-scale research in real-life settings. No previous knowledge of research methods is assumed and the series is particularly suited to practitioners studying for a higher degree or who want to research some aspect of their practice. The thinking underlying the series reflects a major shift in social science research methods over the past fifteen years – away from a natural-sciences style which emphasizes deductive theory-testing, a prior determination of method (usually experimental) and 'generalizable' results, towards a recognition that such requirements are often unworkable and inappropriate in the real world.

This is not a defect, because the traditionally 'scientific' methods are often not adequate as a way of understanding how people behave 'in context'. This does not mean that one should give up an empirical, evidence-based research tradition but adapt to what is possible and, more importantly, what is likely to yield a truer picture.

Bill Gillham

1

Case Study Research: Underlying Principles

What is a case study?

Perhaps we should first ask: what is a *case*? The word 'case' (like 'intelligence' and 'neurosis') is one we all use, and feel we understand, but is rather challenging to define. Here is an attempt:

- a unit of human activity embedded in the real world;
- which can only be studied or understood in context;
- which exists in the here and now;
- that merges in with its context so that precise boundaries are difficult to draw.

A case can be an *individual*: it can be a *group* – such as a family, or a class, or an office, or a hospital ward; it can be an *institution* – such as a school or a children's home, or a factory; it can be a large-scale *community* – a town, an industry, a profession. All of these are single cases; but you can also study *multiple* cases: a number of single parents; several schools; two different professions. It all depends what you want to find out – which leads us on.

A case *study* is one which investigates the above to answer specific research questions (that may be fairly loose to begin with) and which seeks a range of different kinds of evidence, evidence which is there in the case setting, and which has to be abstracted and collated to get the best possible answers to the research questions. No one kind or source of evidence is likely to be sufficient (or sufficiently valid) on its own. This use of multiple sources of evidence, each with its strengths and weaknesses, is a key characteristic of case study research.

Another fundamental characteristic is that you do not start out with *a priori* theoretical notions (whether derived from the literature or not) – because until you get in there and get hold of your data, get to understand the context, you won't know what theories (explanations) work best or make the most sense.

Fundamentals of research

At this point we need to step back and consider some of the underlying principles of research investigation in general, and case study research in particular. It should be noted here that case study research has only recently come into its own, not being part of the natural-sciences style positivist philosophy which in dilute form has dominated the human sciences for so long. In its extreme, original form, positivist philosophers asserted that only observable, and verifiable, phenomena could be the subject matter of science; this excluded subjective phenomena or 'unverifiable' theories. It will be argued below that the naturalistic style of case study research makes it particularly appropriate to study human phenomena, and what it means to be human in the real world 'as it happens'.

Research is about creating new knowledge, whatever the disciplines – history, medicine, physics, social work. The raw material of research is *evidence*, which then has to be made sense of.

In everyday understanding the word 'evidence' is used in two main ways. First, to refer to the findings of 'scientific' research, usually carried out in the form of experiments or other carefully controlled investigations which are presumed to yield 'proven' results of potentially great importance. Note that 'research evidence' for most people equates 'scientific' evidence. Second, the word 'evidence' is used in courts of law and judicial inquiries, as part of the process of judging whether allegations or concerns are likely to be true or not. Much of the process of criminal and civil law is concerned with defining and testing evidence.

One big difference is that 'scientific' evidence is, in a sense, manufactured. It is an outcome of the investigative methods used: it didn't exist before. *Judicial* evidence is there in the case being investigated and has to be uncovered and tested, usually by reasonable argument. Evidence that is a result of the techniques of investigation (for example, asking the wrong kind of questions, or aggressive interviewing) would be disallowed.

The first kind of evidence is natural-sciences style. The natural sciences are those mainly concerned with the material aspects of our world, and the core disciplines are physics and chemistry. Physics is the study of motion and the interactions of matter. Chemistry is the discipline which investigates the properties of natural (and artificial) substances. Both disciplines are concerned with the development of *evidence* and of generalizable *theory* or laws as to how these natural phenomena work. With inanimate substances and their 'activities' scientists can do what they like. Holding some conditions (called 'variables') constant, they manipulate others, to see what results emerge. They may study, for example, the effects of very low temperatures on the molecular structure of steel subjected to different levels of vibration.

Provided there are no dangerous effects, scientists can do as they will with their 'natural' materials. There are no ethical problems and the materials won't complain or try to make sense of what's going on.

With human beings there are great limits to what one can do in manipulating conditions that might affect human behaviour. But even if there were no ethical barriers there are other problems in being objectively 'scientific'.

For example, medical scientists carrying out clinical trials of a new drug have to deal with the placebo effect: the fact that if people believe they are being given a new drug, their symptoms may improve for reasons nothing to do with what they have been given. Medical scientists go to great pains to get round this, at least using double-blind trials, i.e. where the patients don't know what (drug or placebo) they are being given, and the scientists who are actually administering the doses also don't know which one they are giving (so that they can't unwittingly communicate which is which). In a *triple*-blind study, those scientists who assess the improvement in patients from both groups don't know which patients have been given the drug and which not (so that they can't bias the evaluation).

This is an extreme example where the subjects' hopes and expectations are clearly high. But the point is that *all* subjects in experiments are going to have some kind of understanding or expectation of what the experiments are about – and this can affect the results. Experiments work best where the activity is not seen as intrinsically important to the subjects, or where subjects can be treated as *partners* in the investigation. For example, if as a designer you wanted to develop safety bottle caps which young children couldn't operate but weren't too difficult for older people with weak wrists or arthritic hands, you could 'share' your purposes without significantly affecting the results.

But there is a second problem with experiments: in an attempt to get to the fundamental research questions, scientists may 'strip down' the procedures so that they can be carried out under controlled 'laboratory' conditions. Research on memory, until quite recently, has been of this type. The recall of isolated words, or groups of digits, has been tested under various conditions to see how the memory works. One apparently durable finding was that the human memory can hold, at any one time, no more than seven 'bits' of information plus or minus two. However, this is in the laboratory. Human beings are inextricably part of their environment: they may behave differently (not typically or 'normally') in a controlled 'laboratory' setting. For example, an American researcher investigated the phenomenon of short-term memory in cocktail waitresses. He found that these young women, working at speed, could easily remember thirty to forty separate drinks orders at any one time. This is memory working in context with other elements to help recall. (Henry L. Bennett (1983) 'Remembering drinks orders: the memory skills of a cocktail waitress', *Human Learning*, **2**, 157–69.)

Over the past fifteen years there has been a major growth in *ecological psychology* (the study of humans in interaction with their environments): a growth which corresponds with the increased importance of non-experimental case study research. Ecological psychology embodies many of the principles expounded here.

The foregoing has not been an attempt to 'rubbish' experimental research, but rather an attempt to redress the balance. Novice researchers are often obsessed with being 'scientific'; insofar as this means getting good quality evidence and interpreting and checking it in legitimate ways this is laudable. But it is often taken to mean 'hard science' methods – which are often misunderstood and used inappropriately.

Quasi-judicial or 'naturalistic' research

Both 'natural-sciences style' and 'naturalistic' research are legitimate methods of enquiry. You use the methods (and

5

therefore the underlying philosophy) which are best-suited to what you are trying to find out. The key question is: how appropriate is the method to the phenomenon you are dealing with? In other words does the method used mean that important elements are missed out or constrained?

Our argument here is that 'experimental science' type approaches are ill-suited to the complexity, embedded character, and specificity of real-life phenomena.

This last point (specificity) is a key one. Natural sciences research is aimed at *generalizable* findings (which may have general implications for theory). But in human behaviour, generalization from one group of people to others, or one institution to another, is often suspect – because there are too many elements that are *specific* to that group or institution. For example, what is true about one school (e.g. the causes of bullying, or low achievement, or high delinquency rates) may well not be true of another.

Because of this unknown degree of specificity, and the uniqueness of what are likely to be the facts (and how they are to be explained), the naturalistic researcher differs from the experimental investigator in another important way. In the natural-sciences style you study the literature and work out whether existing findings and theories are adequate. If you feel that certain data are not there or that existing theories need testing or challenging, you set up an experimental procedure to yield new data to test existing theory. This is the *deductive* model, using a predetermined procedure of investigation.

The naturalistic researcher cannot work like this: the data and theories in the literature may have little bearing upon the 'case' under investigation. The researcher needs to know what others have done (and their explanations) but cannot be sure they're relevant. The first stage is to review the *context* from which the research questions, the means of investigating them, and likely explanations will emerge. An *emergent* design is characteristic of this style along with *inductive* theorizing, i.e. making sense of what you find after you've found it.

But perhaps the major distinction is the greater concern of naturalistic, case study research with *subjectivity*: with phenomenological meaning. This doesn't mean that you ignore the objective (what people do, what records show, and so on) but that you are after the *qualitative* element: how people understand themselves, or their setting – what lies behind the more objective evidence. Nor does it mean that you ignore 'results' (reading standards in a school, staff turnover in a children's home, after-care of hospital patients) but that you seek to find the *underlying* reasons – in people's feelings or perceptions, or their experiences of what is going on. This concern with *process* (leading to the outcomes or 'results') can be key to understanding what needs to be done to change things.

All of this means that the naturalistic researcher is not a detached 'scientist' but a participant observer who acknowledges (and looks out for) their role in what they discover. A research investigation is not neutral; it has its own dynamic and there will be effects (on individuals, on institutions) precisely because there is someone there asking questions, clarifying procedures, collecting data. Recognizing this is part of doing good research. Ignoring it is bad 'science'.

A lot has been covered in this chapter and it may not be easy to grasp as a whole. The following table summarizes (in what has to be acknowledged as rather artificial opposition) the key differences between the two approaches.

Quasi-natural sciences/ positivist	**Quasi-judicial/ naturalistic**
Emphasis on:	*Emphasis on:*
• experimental methods	• non-experimental methods
• deductive theorizing, i.e. hypothesis testing	• inductive theorizing, i.e. hypothesis seeking
• preordained research design	• emergent research design
• objectivity	• subjectivity
• detachment	• participation
• quantitative data to determine significance of results	• qualitative data to give meaning to results
• significance or otherwise of outcomes	• meaning of processes that lead to outcomes
• demonstration of changes that have occurred	• meaning of changes that have occurred
• generalizable data sought	• generalization regarded as suspect: the context specificity of data is recognized
• isolating the elements of behaviour for investigation	• the importance of context in shaping behaviour
• constructing evidence	• searching for evidence in context

Like all oppositional comparisons the contrasts here are too simple and too strong, but the dimensions of comparison are essentially correct. However, in the chapter that follows the merging or breakdown of the hypothetical barriers will be discussed.

2

Case Study Research: The Qualitative Dimension

'Qualitative' is one of those words that tend to faze people. Students writing in exams sometimes use the words 'qualitative' and 'quantitative' with what is evidently only a hazy notion of their meaning.

Quantitative methods are those which involve counting and measuring: the much-dreaded subject of statistics. Tackling one's anxieties about this is an important task for the novice researcher. Like most objects of anxiety the reality is a good deal less troubling than the anticipation; and once you get to grips with it (even if you are no mathematician) you will find much of it relatively easy and – more important – practically useful. Statistics are of two kinds: *descriptive* and *inferential*. Descriptive statistics are things like averages (usually called 'means') which 'describe' data in a summary fashion. Inferential statistics are those which enable you to draw potentially meaningful and significant inferences from quantitative data. For example, if boys and girls show different proportions of success or failure in an exam, inferential statistics will enable you to say how likely it is that the difference is a 'chance' one, i.e. whether or not it is 'significant'. The chapter on chi square in the companion volume in this series *Developing a Questionnaire* illustrates this kind of technique in some detail, and the later chapter in this book on quantitative methods in case study research takes a wider view. That is all we need to say here about quantitative methods.

Qualitative methods are essentially descriptive and inferential in character and, for this reason, are often seen as 'soft'. But description and inference are also necessary in 'scientific' research. You may have significant statistical results, but these have to be described and *interpreted*: 'facts' do not speak for themselves – someone has to speak for them. And it is here that the quantitative/qualitative distinction starts to break down.

Qualitative methods focus primarily on the kind of evidence (what people tell you, what they do) that will enable you to understand the meaning of what is going on. Their great strength is that they can illuminate issues and turn up possible explanations: essentially a search for meaning – *as is all research*. 'Scientific' researchers, before they run their experiments, will often engage in qualitative-style investigations which lead to hunches about what modifications could be made to existing theory, or how different results from those in the existing literature could be obtained: another part of the blurring of the distinction.

However, before we go further down this road it needs to be emphasized that case study research is not exclusively concerned with qualitative methods: all evidence is pulled into the case study researcher's data collection. However, qualitative methods (and what they enable you to do) are primary.

Thus for the case study researcher all evidence is of *some* value, and this value (trustworthiness) has to be carefully appraised. Reality (and the truth) is not tidy. A judge presiding over a judicial inquiry (as distinct from a court of law) turns no evidence away but assesses what faith can be placed in it, and relates it to other evidence to hand. Broadly speaking, this is the approach of the case study researcher.

What qualitative methods enable you to do

1. To carry out an investigation where other methods – such as experiments – are either not practicable or not ethically justifiable.
2. To investigate situations where little is known about what is there or what is going on. More formal research *may* come later.
3. To explore complexities that are beyond the scope of more 'controlled' approaches.
4. To 'get under the skin' of a group or organization to find out what really happens – the informal reality which can only be perceived from the inside.
5. To view the case from the inside out: to see it from the perspective of those involved.
6. To carry out research into the *processes* leading to results (for example how reading standards were improved in a school) rather than into the 'significance' of the results themselves.

These are strong characteristics and represent a powerful argument for the use of qualitative methods to answer some questions in some settings. But we need to be clear about the philosophical base. There are three main points:

1. Human behaviour, thoughts and feelings are partly determined by their context. If you want to understand people in real life, you have to study them in their context and in the way they operate.
2. 'Objective' research techniques – abstracted, controlling – can produce results that are *artefacts* of the methods used. An artefact is something that only arises because of the method that has been used (like controlled memory experiments in a laboratory or 'opinions' given in a questionnaire). You get results, but are they 'true' for the people concerned in the practice of real life?
3. How people behave, feel, think, can only be understood if

you get to know their world and what they are trying to do in it. 'Objectivity' can ignore data important for an adequate understanding.

What you are looking for in qualitative research

What you are looking for is what *all* researchers in *all* disciplines are concerned with:

- evidence;
- theory.

You need the 'facts' – imperfect though they may be; and you need to be able to understand or explain them (theory).

'Theory' is commonly assumed to be something there and established (Freudian theory, etc.). But theory is something researchers create. It may be that they only modify existing theory, but it may be that they start from scratch. Theories (explanations) derived in that way may be the most generalizable aspect of case study research, i.e. the actual *data* that you find may be specific to a particular school, or factory, or family, or individual, but your *theory* (rooted in what you find) may be useable by other people; or generalizable in understanding how other schools, factories, families or individuals work. Good theories are fertile: they account for a lot of data.

But theory is not primary; evidence is primary. A lot of researchers try cramming their data into an unsuitable theoretical framework; perhaps they don't like to think for themselves...

The case study researcher, working *inductively* from what's there in the research setting develops *grounded theory*: theory that is grounded in the evidence that is turned up.

In the real world evidence is of various kinds and none of it is perfect. It is tempting to rush in (at least in one's head) to analysis and theorizing at too early a stage in the investigation. One must bide one's time; other evidence may qualify, or complicate, or contradict what came early on.

Very broadly, the case study researcher must strive to keep an open mind, to go on looking for data, deferring analysis until the array is comprehensive (and you don't stop completely, even then).

Different data, different methods

Case study is a *main* method. Within it different sub-methods are used: interviews, observations, document and record analysis, work samples, and so on.

Data accumulated by different methods but bearing on the same issue are part of what is called the *multi-method* approach.

Different methods have different strengths and different weaknesses. If they *converge* (agree) then we can be reasonably confident that we are getting a true picture. If they don't agree then we have to be cautious about basing our understanding on any one set of data. That doesn't mean that one set of data is wrong (or any of them) but that the picture is more complicated than we expected.

This approach from different methodological standpoints is usually known as *triangulation*. If they give you the same fix, that's fine. If not, then you have to explain that or question the adequacy of the methods.

A common discrepancy is between what people *say* about themselves and what they actually *do*. In an interview people can be very convincing, because they are sincere. But, as G. K. Chesterton observed in *The Return of Don Quixote*, 'people are never more mistaken about themselves than when they are speaking sincerely and from the heart'. They're not lying; they're just not accurate. In a sense they don't know themselves. So if teachers in a school express a high level of satisfaction in their job, you need to check whether staff turnover, and staff absences, corroborate that. There are commonly discrepancies here. People are similarly inaccurate (but still sincere) about their eating habits.

What you are dealing with here are two things that are quite different: what people *believe* (and it is a fact that they believe what they're saying) and what they actually *do*. To expect them to be the same is to misunderstand how people function. And it means that *theory* has to cope with this complexity.

There is a similar discrepancy in health education which is usually predicated on the assumption that if people know more about health risks and healthy living they will change their behaviour. This is true to some extent for educated adults, but not always then (do you smoke? – if so don't you know why you shouldn't? – and if so why hasn't that changed what you do?). Again what people *know* may have little relation to what they *do*. The complex relationship has to be accounted for by theory. Why do some people act on health advice/information and not others? What is the relationship between rationality and behaviour? Clearly it isn't straightforward: *theory* has to account for that. If people are 'contradictory' that still has to be explained.

3

Research Preliminaries

The essential first steps

In traditional experimental research the first step is to review the literature: to find out what is already known, where it is lacking and what needs to be done to get new evidence to test existing theory. There will be some piloting of methods, some preliminary investigations, much creative reflection, but the main emphasis is as described. Because the aim is to achieve generalizable additions to knowledge which have implications for theory.

The case study researcher faces a rather different situation. His or her 'case' will have unknown and highly specific characteristics. To read the literature *in vacuo* may mean that irrelevant or unsuitable material is studied. And research aims and questions derived from it may have to be abandoned as the live case is taken up.

This is not to say that reading the literature is not important: you will almost certainly learn a great deal that is useful. *But you need to do it in parallel with getting to know your case in context*. From the beginning there needs to be this kind of interaction – a form of dialogue. So your first steps are these:

- reading the (probably) relevant literature;
- getting to know your case or cases in their setting;

- deciding, in a not too focused fashion, what your broad aims are;
- making a start on getting your research questions into shape.

You don't rush into carrying out your actual investigation, because if you do so without adequate time given to these first steps your research will be inadequately based, almost certainly a waste of time.

Everything follows from this first essential stage.

Aims and questions

Most people start their research with a broad aim in mind. They want to find out why more boys than girls truant from secondary school; or why staff on a company training scheme often fail to complete training; or – to pick up a theme from the end of the last chapter – to find out, in a medical general practice, what proportion of patients don't take prescribed drugs properly, and why that is so.

In research, broad aims often remain the same. What changes and evolves is the set of research questions. These emerge in response to asking yourself: what do I need to find out in order to achieve my aim? To take the last example given above, research questions might be: What proportion of patients don't comply with medical advice on drugs? Are there differences (i.e. age, social class) between different categories of patient? Is age a factor? Is the medical condition a factor?

Now you may start off with questions like these but, as you get into the research, as you get to talk to patients, doctors and practice nurses, other questions might emerge, e.g., how clearly are patients told about drug use and the need for compliance? Would follow-up improve compliance? Are patients taking the drugs but not complying with other aspects of medical advice (diet, exercise)?

The point is that the questions *emerge*, and may change radically as you get to know the context at first hand.

The importance of framing your research direction in the form of *questions* is that you are then driven to consider your *methods*: How would I answer those questions? What information do I need and how would I go about getting it?

Framing good questions is the most important part of research procedure. In real-world research they are not easily achieved and you will have to spend quite a long time developing or modifying them. 'Good' research questions are those which will enable you to achieve your aim and which are *capable of being answered in the research setting*. It's no use asking questions that can't be answered.

In the real world there are always constraints on what the researcher can do – ethical, practical (in particular avoiding making life difficult for people who have many other things to contend with). So you have to perform a balancing act between what you want to find out and what the setting will allow you to do. There is a positive side to this: there may be unrealized potentialities. A real example occurred in a research project led by the author, which was looking at the use of volunteer tutors with failing readers in the first two years of the primary school. It is easy to demonstrate short-term effects with this kind of intervention – but does it last? In the course of the research (which was to run for several years) we found that the school had their own longitudinal data on reading trends in the *third* year of the school. Thus we were able to plot changes, more than a year after the learning support ended, with a sequence of pre-intervention baseline scores, i.e. those third years who hadn't had the intervention, with those in successive years who had. Because of that potentiality we were able to ask questions about follow-up effects that we hadn't thought possible.

Keeping an open mind

The broad strategy in case study research is to start by collecting data (and looking for it) with as open a mind as possible. A particular difficulty here is that we all carry a lot of conceptual baggage with us. We 'know' what it's like to be an office worker or a teacher, or a GP, or whatever. Well, we know what it was like for us and, being human, we can easily assume that that gives us privileged understanding of others in similar contexts. This very familiarity can blind us and close our minds.

You need to take the stance that you are going into a foreign country. In the 1920s, a cultured Swiss, L. S. Renier, recorded his impressions of the English in a famous book, *The English: Are They Human?*. It is a highly instructive read.

Renier was able to see the English with uncomfortable clarity because he knew quite well they were different from himself. Accordingly he didn't make assumptions – of familiarity or similarity that another Englishman might. So even if you 'know' the setting you have to act as if you didn't: *because you don't*.

When you move your job (within the same profession) it can be very surprising how an ostensibly similar school, hospital, office or factory is profoundly different from what you've experienced, once you get to know it. Indeed some of your initial settling-in difficulties may be because of assumptions you've made (almost unconsciously).

The researcher needs to be alert to this from the beginning. The stance needs to be that of social anthropologists going to study a culture quite different from their own. The framework they take with them is a strategy for gathering evidence – detailed evidence, the significance of which (or otherwise) will only gradually emerge. Analysis, sorting, categorizing and theorizing must be deferred for the moment.

That is not easy. A basic limitation of human cognition is

that we feel impelled to understand, to make sense of what we are experiencing. New knowledge is mainly interpreted in terms of what we already know, until that proves so inadequate that our 'knowledge framework' undergoes a radical reorganization. In research this is sometimes known as a *paradigm* shift – a complete change in the way we understand or theorize about what we are studying.

The American social anthropologist Clifford Geertz emphasizes the importance of beginning research into any culture by *describing* what you find in some detail. He calls this *thick description*: a process which makes you pay attention to the fine grain of what you are observing, and reflecting on it. We are now getting to the central concern of the case study method: the collection and study of multiple forms of evidence, in sufficient detail to achieve understanding.

4

Evidence: The Primary Concern

All evidence is of some use to the case study researcher: nothing is turned away. It will vary in relevance or trustworthiness or completeness (but you won't know to begin with). You accumulate. Because this can easily get untidy – and difficult to access – you need to be organized in this respect, mainly by sorting out *types* of evidence (see below). So, *Point One*, you need to maintain a *case study database* (from which the report will be written following analysis).

Point Two is that you must be alert to the need for *multiple sources of evidence*. This doesn't just mean talking to a lot of different people (although you should do that, and cross-refer) but that you should look for different *kinds* of evidence: what people *say*, what you see them *doing*, what they *make* or *produce*, what documents and records *show*.

In the end, all of this evidence needs to be woven into a narrative account presenting what Yin in *Case Study Research: Design and Methods* (1989) calls a *chain of evidence*, i.e. each key element or link in your account supported by or related to evidence of different kinds.

Different kinds of evidence

It is useful to have a list of the main types of evidence because it is easy to neglect one kind or source. These are the main headings:

1. *Documents*. These can be letters, policy statements, regulations, guidelines. They provide a formal framework to which you may have to relate the informal reality – for example, if you are investigating safety in the workplace.
2. *Records*. These are the things that go back in time but may provide a useful longitudinal fix on the present situation. For example: the number and kinds of accidents reported in the workplace; time off work as a result of injury, etc. These may well be stored on computer files.
3. *Interviews*. This is an inadequate term for the range of ways in which people can give you information. This may be more informal than an interview, for example an off-the-cuff spontaneous discussion. Or more formal, such as a brief questionnaire (not usual in case studies, but not out of the question – no pun intended).
4. *'Detached' observation*. This is the 'fly on the wall' approach and very different from 'participant' observation. Its main use is where you need to be more systematic in how you observe. See chapter 7 on observation.
5. *Participant observation*. This is the more usual sort in a case study – where you are 'in' the setting in some active sense – perhaps even working there (and there is nothing to stop you doing a case study of where you work) but keeping your ears and eyes open, noticing things that you might normally overlook. An important part of this kind of data collection is keeping a written record (see pp. 23ff).
6. *Physical artefacts*. These are things made or produced. Samples of children's academic work, for example. If you were doing a multiple case study of dyslexic students, then samples of their written work could be an important part of your data collection. Sometimes this kind of evidence is the most important. If you were studying creativity in designers you might keep actual samples or photographic

records of, for example, sketches, mock-ups, materials used, prototypes, and so on.

Why this evidence is so important

The basic way of presenting a case study report is a narrative following the logic and chronology of your investigation and reasoning. In a sense that is true of all scientific papers: they have a 'narrative' sequence and 'tell a story', although they are rarely a compelling read. But the case study researcher, who is seeking to recreate the context and sequence of evidence in a way that enables the reader to see and understand the meaning of what is recounted, has to use a more overtly narrative format. Well done, these can be compellingly readable; but they are open to the criticism (sour grapes?) that they are nothing much more than a good story. Well, the truth can be a good story, though not usually a very tidy one, and presenting this well does call for some literary skill – of a plain, straightforward kind. But at each key point in the narrative – and continuously in an interwoven fashion – evidence needs to be presented for the development and direction of the narrative. This must be much more than impressionistic: impressions and assertions must be substantiated in some way.

Here we are anticipating the outcome of the study, but it is to make the point that the ability to do that depends upon the maintenance of organized and detailed records throughout the project. Record-keeping is of various kinds, but there is one element that is crucial.

Maintaining a research log

Here is where we take a leaf from the social anthropologist's book.

A research log can be electronic but it is still more usual to maintain a 'manual' one: a flip-over secretarial pad is ideal. This goes with you everywhere. In it you put down two main kinds of things:

- *Evidence* of one kind or another: a discussion you've heard in a staffroom; a comment made to you; something you've observed (e.g. a worker by-passing a required safety procedure). These may be fragmentary, unrepresentative, but they *occurred*: so they're evidence. You need to follow this up: are they typical, are they true, etc.?
- *Personal notes*: questions you need to reflect on; insights, hunches or ideas; a report you hear mentioned that you need to get a copy of; the name of someone you need to consult; statistics you need to check; and so on.

A log book is necessarily summary in the main (not always: sometimes you will feel the need to record observations in depth and at length). Entries are best made immediately: a habit that will save you a lot of trouble. In any case, writing things down, even very summarily, has a curiously clarifying and focusing effect on the mind. It is part of research discipline.

Your log is in a sense a private thing, but it is more than that. You need to take the stance that all of your research records (and what they show) are open for inspection; organized but not 'tidied' so that someone else could follow the process of the investigation. This notion of 'open accounting' is partly an ethical stance – demonstrating your reasoning and the chain of evidence on which it is based. But it is also of great practical value when you come to write up your report. When you are busily 'in' the research activity and things are moving fast (research questions and explanations developing rapidly) it is easy to lose sight of where you've come from: yet this is a key dimension of the research process.

The log book is more than a set of rough notes: it is a fundamental part of your database, and needs to be treated with respect. It is also the beginning of what Guba and Lincoln, pioneers in naturalistic research, call the 'audit trail' – something that an 'auditor' could follow to understand your procedures (see *Effective Evaluation* (1981), San Francisco: Jossey Bass).

So, you carefully preserve your log books. But you do more than that. Because they are often hastily written by hand it is good discipline to do a *daily* and *exact* transcription onto a word processor taking care to date and number each day. You could if you wish then *colour code* the contents, particularly the 'evidence' and 'personal' notes, and separate them into distinct manual files – especially important for the 'evidence' notes.

You will then have your 'field notes' available to yourself and others in legible, readily accessible format.

At the end of each week, or whatever interval seems appropriate, you need to read through your notes and review what you've turned up. What you then have to do is to prepare a summary of:

- the different types of evidence you've uncovered;
- what your immediate priorities for action are;
- any reworking of your research aims and questions;
- your 'theorizing': what you think this might be about, how it might be explained.

If you do regular summaries like this you will be able to plot the progression of your thinking when you come to write your report.

Reviewing and summarizing is essential to the discipline of case study research: a kind of intellectual stocktaking. It needs to be done regularly and systematically – only in that way will you maintain the necessary level of control over the process. Case study research can easily 'lose shape' because of the complexity of the material.

Once a month you should do a major review of progress and write a progress report (for your own records and perhaps for others) of what you've achieved and how your research design and theory have developed.

As the data collection progresses (and accumulates) you will move from gathering data to making more focused, selective decisions about what you are going to concentrate on. For example, you may have started out looking at the whole picture of bullying in a school but, because it has emerged as a neglected dimension, decide to focus on bullying that occurs on the way to school and which appears to be a factor in school absences.

Decisions of this kind need to be recorded (and justified) in your review records.

Data *analysis* procedures (how you're going to order and present your findings) become increasingly important as the investigation moves on. At some point data collection has to virtually stop and will have been winding down for some time before that. Somehow you have to reduce this mass of data. There are standard techniques for analysing different kinds of data – these are described in the chapters that follow dealing with particular kinds of evidence. But in the same way that case study evidence may be specific or peculiar to the case in question, analysis also has to be appropriate and not a straightjacket that deforms your findings. This may mean that you have to be creative about your methods of analysis. Bear in mind that the purpose of analysis is to faithfully reflect in summary and organized form what you have found.

A key term in naturalistic research is 'trustworthiness'. Although there have been fraudulent researchers, there is little real satisfaction in methods and 'findings' that lack integrity. But interpreting research data is more than a matter of good intentions. It requires discipline and concentration to present a 'true' picture: anything that gets in the way of that threatens the validity of your research.

Reality – a reflection of the real world that your case

inhabits – is unlikely to be tidy and may appear 'contra-dictory'. Don't feel that you have to 'clean up' the picture to make it acceptable. We return to this point in the next chapter.

5

Evidence: What to Look Out For

Human intelligence is by its nature selective. If William James was right (and he was less right than he thought), babies are born into a 'blooming, buzzing confusion'. Actually they are crudely selective right from the start; and they rapidly get better at it. If we didn't select from all the things around us we should be overwhelmed by them.

In that sense, then, an 'open mind' is impossible. And in case study research the researcher is the (human) research instrument.

But there is a level of 'closed-mindedness' that we can deal with, and that is our preconceptions and expectations: in a word our *prejudices*. These are pre-judgements of things we don't know or don't know much about, epitomized in the famous Guinness advert, 'I've never tried it because I don't like it'. Prejudices are normal, and most of them are of little importance (it's no moral crime not to drink Guinness).

It's human and normal to come to the research process with prejudices. But you need to ask yourself constantly: What do I *expect* to find? What do I think this is all about? These are your prejudices. You may be right. Prejudices aren't necessarily wrong: they're just based on inadequate evidence. More sinister than prejudices, however, are our *preferences*. Not just what you expect to find, but what you *want* to find. Ask yourself: what do I hope to uncover here? What is the preferred picture as far as I am concerned?

When you read research papers you can often see that people have found what they *wanted* to find. Which is hardly surprising. But researchers of integrity are constantly challenging and scrutinizing themselves. And the first stage in that process is to get your expectations and preferences out into the open. You acknowledge them. You write them down. They are as much a part of the research process as anything else. 'Objectivity' in the absolute sense may be an impossibility but that doesn't mean that you immerse yourself in an uncritical subjectivity. You strive for a level of detached honesty which acknowledges your own place in the scheme of things. In a sense, you *de*centre from yourself. There are a number of ways in which you go about this.

Absorbing the culture

This is the heavy emphasis at the beginning of the research process; and it never entirely stops.

You go in with your eyes and your ears open: you look and you listen. What's it like to be a pensioner subsisting on the basic state pension? What's it like to work in a fast-food outlet? What's it like to work in an open-plan office the size of a factory floor? What's it like to be a probationer teacher in an inner-city school? You can only find out by spending time with people in their setting. In a sense each location has its own culture: the conventions by which it works. It also has its own values and 'language' – ways of judging and thinking and talking about the living experience.

It takes time to penetrate that. Not least because we all have a 'front' – which we may believe in – that we present to outsiders. The value of being a participant observer, perhaps becoming a temporary member of the setting, is that you are more likely to get to the informal reality. Outsiders of a perceived high or official status may never get there. Trainee teachers, for example, may get a better view of how a school works than a visiting inspector.

Looking for discrepant data

As you proceed you acquire a lot of information and you develop provisional explanations. But are there data that don't fit these 'theories' that you are developing? Looking for negative, i.e. opposite or contradictory, evidence, or evidence that qualifies or complicates your emerging understanding, is basic to research integrity. The temptation is to close your mind, to think that you've 'got it'. For example, you may have decided that the management in a factory are not to be blamed for violation of safety procedures because they hold regular safety training programmes for workers, so that it is a matter of individual worker responsibility or irresponsibility. But as you continue to watch what people on the shop floor do you may see that the training is not suited to the practical requirements of doing the job – so that workers take short-cuts to keep to schedule – and that shop-floor supervision largely disregards safety procedures except for a temporary increase in concern and rigour following an accident.

Triangulation: taking different bearings

A constant theme in this book is that different kinds of data (or different sources) bearing on the same issue commonly yield contradictory or 'discrepant' results. If every kind of evidence agrees then you have simple, confirmatory triangulation. If what people say, and what they do, and what records show all concur then you have a straightforward picture.

Often you don't get that. The straightforward 'fix' doesn't

apply. It doesn't mean that one set of data is 'untrue', rather that the presumed relationship with the triangulation point either doesn't exist or has to be understood differently.

A lot of things that make straightforward sense, super-ficially, can be shown by research not to be or not to operate as you expected. To take the work safety example: if a company was concerned about the rising number of shop-floor accidents, they might set up training programmes as a means of combating the problem. There are archival records of accident rates over several years. Do rates change after training is initiated? This kind of analysis is called *time-series* or *pattern* analysis. If rates do go down is that due to the training? Maybe.

But you would have to look at other possible causes. Perhaps shop-floor supervisors have got the message that this is a high priority for the management, so they are more vigilant. Workers may feel that carelessness could lead to dismissal and so on. Different 'bearings' may qualify the picture.

The representativeness of data

Representativeness is different from triangulation. You listen to what people tell you, but are you listening only to some people? Or, to put it another way, is it that some people – knowing you are the 'observer' – are keen to get their case across to you? If people want to 'help' you, you need to ask yourself: why? Those who are more cautious may have a quite different picture to present – either because they are more private in their habits or because they know that what they think does not fit the party line. So, is what you're getting representative of all shades of opinion?

This is the issue of 'accessibility'. In any area some kinds of information, some people, are more accessible than others. So that kind of data, the opinions of those people, are disproportionately apparent. This is one of the weaknesses of journalism where (usually) the most quickly accessible is what gets published. But that doesn't mean that the picture presented is comprehensive or representative.

Whatever the kind of evidence (documents and records, what people say, what they do, the physical or social context they inhabit) an adequate picture involves a lot of digging away. Even published documents, for example, go largely unread, or are read without an appreciation of their significance. Not all publications are high profile. The stuff is there but it isn't known. Important data are not necessarily readily accessible, lying there on the surface, so to speak.

This is true even with the people who are eager to talk to you. The psychiatrist Harry Stack Sullivan, in one of his published lectures on the psychiatric interview, commented that the most important thing to note is not what people tell you about, but what they avoid telling you about.

So there may be parts of an organization that tend to be overlooked, aspects of professional practice that are not acknowledged, and so on. You have to be alert to these limits, and to the signs of what is there but not visible.

Asking yourself how you know things

This topic links into the preceding one, but focuses on how researchers come to know their evidence. We know what we know. But knowledge is either *tacit* or *explicit*. If it's explicit we can explain how and why we know it, i.e. we can cite the evidence. Tacit knowledge (sometimes called intuition) is where we sense or feel something, often very strongly, but are hard put to explain or justify. There is nothing wrong with intuitive knowledge: your antennae may have picked up something important which needs exploring.

For example, a head teacher may be telling you about the school policy and practice in relation to racism in her school,

31

how racist incidents are dealt with, and so on. She is fluent and coherent; but somehow you don't entirely believe it.

You need to ask yourself two questions:

- why? i.e. what doesn't ring true?
- how would I check out what I've been told?

You neither accept your intuition as some magical divination of the truth nor reject it because it isn't hard-and-fast evidence.

Case study research is very much like detective work. Nothing is disregarded: everything is weighed and sifted; and checked or corroborated.

Checking your ideas and explanations with those in the culture

You can do this in various ways. It may be that you give a presentation to the people in the setting where you are working. This can be important for various reasons. A lot of people will have given you help of one kind or another. Perhaps others are curious as to just what you are up to. Of course, you should be explaining the purpose of your research, informally, whenever the opportunity presents itself. But that can be a scrappy and incoherent process. Also a specially prepared presentation signals your wish to communicate, inform – and *consult*.

Telling them what you're doing is one thing; asking them what they think is another. You can turn such a presentation into something like a focus group discussion. There is much to benefit you in the business of presenting a summary report; but most important is to test out your provisional *understanding* or explanations of what it's all about. And you present this by saying: this is what it means to me, this is how I make sense of it. What do *you* think? Can you put me right?

You'll get immediate feedback but you will also have

sensitized individuals to what you're about. Some of those, on reflection, will perhaps come to you with their further thoughts.

It may be that you need to set up a regular consultation group – particularly if what you are doing has, or could have, policy implications: again it serves the dual purpose of keeping your 'hosts' informed; and getting feedback from them.

Finally, there may be other key individuals (not necessarily in formal positions of power) whom you could consult: perhaps thoughtful, experienced or committed individuals who are experts on the context you are investigating. It is more likely that you will have to seek them out than that they seek you out.

Peer consultation

Your peers are other people like you: other students, other researchers, your supervisor. These are the ones who are doing the same kind of thing as yourself, are experts in the kind of research you are undertaking, or are experts in research methods. They can save you a lot of trouble. Good supervision, in particular, is of paramount importance as research can be a curiously lonely business. A formal research degree is different from an undergraduate degree because you are not following a formal taught course at the level of subject *content* – although you will normally have *methods* lectures or seminars. In a sense you have to write your own curriculum and you are the only one studying it.

If you are following a structured research degree programme then you will have the support of fellow students, though each is following his or her own research topic. But *methods* may be in common and, of course, your exact peers are at the same level as yourself. Their feedback and shared understanding has a special quality of its own. That is why course tutors regularly organize sessions for each student to present a summary of their research to their peers.

Finding others who have done the same kind of research as yourself, i.e. on the same topic, is more troublesome but can be uniquely rewarding – particularly if they are prepared to talk to you. From them you can get specific guidance and insights into the informal side of researching the topic of the kind that doesn't usually get published.

Your supervisor (if you have one) is likely to know a lot about the broad area of research you are engaged in – without being expert on your specific topic. Perhaps more importantly, they will be expert on the *style* of research that you are doing. The tutorial approach is to get you to summarize, explain, justify, question what you are doing. Over time this has a powerfully disciplining effect on your thinking. You will not usually be told exactly what to do, although your supervisor will indicate acceptable and unacceptable procedures; rather your research programme will be *questioned* into shape.

Theory-building and the analysis of negative evidence

It is an axiom of scientific philosophy that theories cannot be proved – in a definitive sense – only *disproved*. That is, you've got a theory that 'explains' all the evidence, and then something comes along – another piece of unarguable evidence – which doesn't fit the theory: which has to change.

That is what was meant when we said earlier that theory is not primary, evidence is primary; and that applies to all kinds of research.

Good scientists, good researchers, are always testing their assumptions, positively looking out for evidence that challenges their understanding. The alternative is only to look for *confirmatory* evidence: evidence that confirms what you believe or understand. You can see that process in everyday life: people being selective about what they come across, to reinforce their beliefs.

This is the obverse of being a good researcher and is why, on page 29, we suggested that you challenge yourself as to what you expect or hope to find. Research that is ideologically driven (e.g. by moral or political beliefs *however worthy*) is always at risk of being bad research, because contrary evidence may either be discounted or interpreted in a way that fits the belief system.

In naturalistic case study research, theorizing *emerges*. That is because you cannot usefully theorize in the absence of evidence, or on very little. The evidence you look at is initially dictated by your broad aims. But increasingly it is directed by your successively revised theories or explanations. And it is *negative* or complicating evidence that precipitates these revisions.

You may not think of yourself as a theorist. But we construct theories (understandings, explanations) in everyday life about other people. For example, when someone we know well behaves in an unexpected way that we don't understand, what they have done is to give us evidence that challenges our 'theory' about them. And it is the new evidence that makes us realize what we understood them to be like. That is a fortuitous incident: research is a more deliberate process. Let us take a practical but hypothetical example.

In an FE college there is concern about the high drop-out rate from a computing course; in particular, that female students leave at a higher rate than male students. All the tutors are male: is sexism rearing its ugly head? A tentative 'theory' there.

Looking at records you find that female students have lower grades for maths in their entry qualifications. Perhaps they lack the necessary ability? But when you do an analysis

35

(statistics are appropriate here) of grades in GCSE maths and drop-out rate you find that women with good maths grades are just as likely to drop out as those with poor ones, but that this is not true for male students. So your 'theory' has to adapt again: maths ability is relevant for males, not for females.

From group discussions and interviews it becomes apparent that *all* students feel their tutors are helpful and supportive: no hint of sex discrimination here. That explanation is discarded. But *attitudes* to computing, and computing careers, show major differences between the sexes. Female students tend not to want a career that is 'just about computers' and so tend to transfer to other courses where computing skills are involved, but not central. Some kind of working explanation has been arrived at. Not, of course, that it is the last word.

This (fictional) example is enough to illustrate how the broad aims, and the evidence, and the theorizing all interact to give your research direction.

You need to record this process conscientiously: it will be a key part of your final research report.

6

Written and Electronically Stored Material

To avoid cumbersome usage we'll call all of this 'written' evidence, even if some of it has to be printed out.

Written evidence is of two basic kinds: *published* evidence of what other researchers have done or found, or relevant government or other official publications, e.g. statistical reports – part of the external context that your case inhabits. And the usually *unpublished* documents and records that are found mainly in institutions (though individuals may have their own documentation which may be relevant – for example, of how they spend their income).

The published literature

It is useful to do some reading round your research topic before you go into the actual setting, but the notion that you do an extensive literature review first from which you derive an hypothesis to test is a nonsense in real-world research. It represents an adherence to an inappropriate paradigm.

But nor do you take the stance that your case is so unique that you have nothing to learn from what other researchers have done or think. There can be no simple translation of their findings or theories but there will always be elements which will sharpen your insight into what you're about.

The two processes (getting to know the literature and getting to know your case) should go along simultaneously so that your reading and what you are turning up in your case study *interact*: they feed into each other.

To a great extent you won't know what you're looking for in the literature until you *do* get into the real context. And what you find in the literature will sensitize your perceptions. This progressive influence is one dimension of the emergent character of case study research.

Computer-based searches

Literature-searching is as much art as science. But computer-based searches have made the researcher's life immeasurably easier. They work best when your research topic fits one or two of the main databases. These are usually available in university or college libraries that subscribe to the service (at enormous cost); and in technologically advanced institutions they are available campus-wide or even to distance-learners. Some databases are only available on CD-ROM, but these have declined in importance over the past five years. In any case, some special training in use is required. Research librarians can be a great help here, especially in university libraries. There is a particular mind-set for this kind of thing, apart from 'knowing the ropes'.

The major databases involve reviewers reading and abstracting from an enormous range of journals within one discipline or sub-discipline. This is expensive, which is why subscriptions to these systems are correspondingly costly. To access them you use keywords (in the database's 'dictionary') either alone or usually in combination. The computer then trawls either titles or summaries to see where these keywords co-occur. The more keywords you use the more 'selective' the computer is. For example, if you just put the keyword 'bullying' into the main educational database (ERIC) you would get thousands of citations. But if your interest was in bullying by girls then you could key in 'girls' or 'females' or 'gender' which would cut the range, and focus more on your topic.

What the computer doesn't do is *think* for you, and you may get some very strange titles coming up just because your keywords appear in them.

Most computer systems will first tell you how many titles fit your keywords. There may be so many that you have to think round ways of pruning the number. This is where specialist librarians can be a great help: it may not be their subject area, but they know how the system works and how to render it manageable. When the number looks feasible you can instruct the computer to print out. This will usually give you title and publication details and a summary.

Go through these, highlighting the papers you would like a copy of (be sparing: you have to read them!).

What you are doing is a progressive focusing. A computer search gives you a first quick fix. If we assume that you select half-a-dozen papers you then have something to start on.

However, finding the references is one thing; getting hold of the actual papers is quite another. If the journals or books are in the library you're using then they are immediately accessible. But there are an enormous number of journals, and library subscriptions to them are expensive. A university library's serials budget is usually much more than its books budget. Even then they have to be highly selective.

In the UK almost all journals are held at the British Lending Library at Wetherby Spa. To get a copy of a paper you have to put in an inter-library loan request: and these are expensive. An intermediate step, however, is to find out whether another university or college or public library holds the journal you're interested in. In which case you can get a copy directly from there. There are sometimes local databases which will tell you which libraries hold which journals.

Manual databases and other sources

Computer-based searches are a phenomenon of the last twenty years or so. Before that time one had to use enormous indexed volumes, usually classified under sub-headings but also cross-referenced in various ways. These can still be useful – especially browsing through the titles listed under various sub-headings. Indeed *all* sources turn up something different. No system or approach is complete or infallible. A frustrating but typical experience is that you can be well into a project before you find an absolutely key reference.

Other sources are:

- Browsing through the contents lists of the main journals in your topic area. Always start with the most recent one (because if you find a paper it will give references to earlier ones) and go back about five years. You'll find that you can do this quite quickly.
- Looking through the bibliographies in books on your topic. These can be very extensive, with references going back a long way. Photocopy the pages and highlight the references you want to pursue. You can do the same with the occasional, very lengthy *review* papers which you may find in journals.
- Talking to experienced researchers in your area. In some ways this can be the most valuable source of all: a source that is intelligent, that can answer questions and, most important, can challenge and direct you. They will have been through the searching process that you are starting – and will have gone a long way beyond it. Write to them, explaining what you are doing and ask if you can come to see them. *Don't* send detailed questions which will require a lengthy written reply: these are the bane of specialist academics. In any case you'll find a face-to-face meeting richer and more helpful. It will be worth the trip.

Analysing and organizing the literature

The journal papers (or whatever) that you've copied, or those you have sent for, are to hand. How do you proceed?

The first step is to read each paper through quickly (not too many at one time or you'll suffer mental indigestion) *highlighting* key points or passages. These are the elements you feel are most important or which contain something you have some further use for. In the text, reference will be made to other publications that you may want to follow up: highlight these and, when you've read the paper, go through the reference list at the end highlighting those papers that you want to get hold of.

This is how searching proceeds – like an inverted tree diagram where one paper (the 'stem') leads into other 'branches' – which then lead you on to the references cited there. To a considerable degree the published literature is interlinked so that, to use another metaphor, when you pick up one thread, others are joined to it.

Gradually you accumulate your references. What you will usually find is that a small number of them is much more central or useful than others. The process is one of sorting.

And because you're researching the real-life context at the same time, what's important progressively becomes more apparent. The interaction is an interesting one of intellectual discovery. What you read makes you look out for things in your research context; what you find there makes you read papers with a different eye.

At some point – not too early – you should attempt a literature review. You'll need this for your final report anyway but you should see it also as a means of clarifying things for yourself. It's a skill all of its own and the only way to learn it is to do it. A first draft will be unsatisfactory but successive revisions will become increasingly balanced and representative. It isn't just the balance of writing that improves: your *thinking* does. Writing is a primary discipline for clarifying what's in your mind.

Researching the 'unpublished' literature

Published, or publicly available, documents and records help you to appraise the wider context that your case inhabits. But there is a more local literature context. Institutions in particular will have their own literature which is usually neither published nor available to the public. Some of it is generally available by its very nature – school handbooks for parents, for example. And large organizations or professional groups will probably have a range of public documents as part of their public relations function. These are likely to be more or less idealized – presenting their best face to clients or customers. This formal representation should not be taken as an accurate account of the informal reality. However, in a case study, they are part of the evidence, even if their relationship to other kinds of evidence is not straightforward.

It is useful to make a distinction between:

- *documents*: policy statements, minutes of meetings, reports of one kind or another;
- *records*: often computer stored: detailing absence rates, turnover, changes in numbers (employed or on roll), accidents, and so on.

Locating documents

Because in a group or organization or profession, documents may not be part of a reference system, learning about their existence (and locating them) may not be straightforward. This is where *communicating* what it is you are trying to find out to members of the group is important. If people know what you're after they may be able to guide you. Some individuals will be key informants. In a sense they have their own mental referencing system. One invaluable source can be secretarial office staff, who will have word-processed and filed many of these documents. Their understanding and helpfulness can be crucial; but remember to check with the management before asking staff to copy documents for you.

Document search and analysis (a main method if you are an historian) epitomizes the case study research strategy. These documents were not drawn up to answer your research questions: but they're part of the evidence base. They are not of course to be taken as representative of what actually happens – the informal reality. But they bear some relation to it: exactly what, you have to discover. What weight you attach to them in your research depends on their relevance to your questions. But that they exist at all is of some significance.

Again, highlighting key passages will help in your later retrieval of the elements you may want to make use of.

Some documents may not be part of the general scene. For example, in a large school you may come to hear of a small group – members of staff – who work together informally on, for example, providing support for female students in subject areas where they traditionally do less well. They may have carried out small surveys, or written their own reports. And these may or may not be relevant to your research. But you need to be alert to the possibility.

Getting access to records (archival data)

Statistics and summary information are maintained for a variety of reasons – usually nothing to do with research *per se*. These can go back several years and so provide a dimension that you could not hope to create for yourself. Getting into these records may present some problems. For example:

- *formal/ethical*: permission and approval for access and use;
- *technical*: they may be part of a computerized retrieval system that you can't (or aren't allowed to) operate;
- *data format*: the data may not be in a form you can easily use or make sense of;
- *data quality*: accuracy and completeness.

You can spend much time and effort overcoming these difficulties, so you need to be clear that it's going to be worth the effort. It *can* be. Interesting findings often emerge from a researcher's painstaking analysis of official or other statistics; and getting round the constraints of the way the statistics are organized so as to extract answers of value is often testimony to a researcher's ingenuity. The key thing to bear in mind is that the database was not designed to answer your questions. But then that is true of much of the evidence that is dealt with in case study research.

'Relevance' comes from weighing and assessing and selecting the evidence that *does* have a bearing on the research issues.

7

Observation: Looking and Listening

When we go into a new social situation, one where we don't know the people or the *mores*, it is the sensible thing to keep a low profile, to watch how other people behave before plunging in with our own contribution. Not to do so may mean that one gets off on the wrong foot, perhaps committing an irretrievable blunder.

This is even more important for the naturalistic researcher. He or she also has to gain social acceptance through sensitivity to and awareness of what is appropriate behaviour. But, unlike in the normal social process, the researcher remains more in the social background even when they are 'participant'. They have to earn their place (like anyone else), but it is not necessarily or usually in the foreground. It doesn't mean being a 'fly on the wall'. Detached observation (see below) has its place, but usually a minor one in naturalistic research.

What is observation?

Very simply observation has three main elements:

- watching what people do;
- listening to what they say;
- sometimes asking them clarifying questions.

Observation is of two main kinds:

- *participant*: being involved – mainly descriptive, i.e. *qualitative*;
- *detached/structured*: watching from 'outside' in a carefully timed and specified way – counting and classifying what you see, i.e. *quantitative*.

These two forms of observation are quite different – opposite ends of the observation dimension – and should be seen as essentially different techniques, yielding different kinds of data. But you don't have to choose one or the other. In the same way that there are different ways of getting people to tell you things – and you can use more than one of them – so you can mix participant/detached observation.

In a case study they constitute just part of the data-collecting techniques. But low-key participant observation is the one you use first: the getting-to-know phase of the research. Structured observation comes later, when you have the research issues well in focus. At that point you'll be able to see where the clarifying (but time-consuming and trouble-some) function of structured observation could yield useful data. It is a technique not to be undertaken lightly.

Observation: pros and cons

The overpowering validity of observation is that it is the most direct way of obtaining data. It is not what people have *written* on the topic (what they intend to do, or should do). It is not what they *say* they do. It is what they *actually* do (which may also be reflected to some extent in records). Its very reality can be overwhelming so that you may easily suspend your critical faculties (like asking: is what I am seeing/ hearing typical or representative of this person or this role or situation?). For the novice researcher observation can seem a very simple business (because it is 'obvious' and because you've 'seen' it). Unfortunately research on 'witnessing' – what people have seen and what they report – shows that observation is both fallible and highly selective. Becoming anything like an accurate and balanced observer requires discipline and effort. And because for the case study researcher the technique is primary – where you start, and where the clues for using other techniques are often turned up – it may be the starting point for error or selective bias.

From the point of view of positivist 'objectivity' a major objection to unstructured participant observation is the effect of your presence on those you are observing. If, as a researcher, you work as part of the team in a children's home you are bound to make a difference: it would be an indictment of you if you didn't. You don't deal with the 'observer effect' by denying it: you look out for the probable influence of your presence. In real-world research as we have mentioned before, the researcher is the research instrument, and any instrument used makes some contribution, has some effect on what is found. You have to make a consistent effort to observe yourself and the effects you might be having. You can also ask members of the group or institution whether they think that what happens when you *are* there is characteristic. A conscious attempt at rigour can usually lead to a reasonable judgement: we can expect no more.

The *observer effect* can be judged a little more precisely in structured observation because you can ask someone else to check on your observations – using the same schedule and perhaps even at the same time – so as to calculate inter-observer reliability. More on that later.

A major problem with observation of whatever kind is that it is time-consuming. Getting to know your case – whether individual or institutional – is necessarily a slow process. Observing people is slower than asking them about what they do. The point at issue is the cross-validity of different kinds of evidence (fundamental to case study method) and the primary validity of observation as a technique. In short, if you want to do case study research you have to be prepared to commit the time to it.

The data from observation are also troublesome to collate and analyse, and difficult to write up adequately, but this is where your research discipline will help. If you write up your observations *as soon as possible* they will be easier to recall and also more accurately recorded. Memory 'improves' – simplifies and selects – the more time it is given to work. Which is why a police officer's contemporaneous notes are seen as more valid than a later, 'tidied' version.

The uses of observation

The use of observation as a technique varies according to the kind of case you are dealing with and the kind of research questions you are asking. If your study involves young children or older people with severe communication difficulties then observation of them is going to be more productive than trying to interview them. If you are researching ethical standards in a profession then talking to members of that group is going to be primary. In other words, the balance of methods within a case study will always vary – according to what is feasible and according to what you want to find out.

Observation can be used in these various ways:

- As an *exploratory* technique. This is the low-profile beginning we mentioned earlier. Experimental psychologists may well start in this way having versed themselves in the literature. But they will be looking for the constraints and potentialities for the methods they prefer. In a broad sense that is entirely analogous with the case study researcher: which directions and methods are appropriate or possible here?
- As an *initial phase* where other methods will take over. Here observation is not viewed as part of the potential

battery of methods, or comes to be seen as inappropriate or too time-consuming. This is an important decision, and one to be weighed carefully. It may be that this assumption has to be modified later when its potentialities become more apparent.

- As a *supplementary* technique to give the illustrative dimension. This is not as superficial a usage as it might seem – no more superficial than well-chosen visual illustrations in a text. This can be particularly potent when the case study is used as a complement to *survey* techniques, i.e. involving hundreds or thousands of individuals or groups or institutions, data that are wide-scale and representative but hard to translate into specific human terms.

- As part of a *multi-method* approach. This is at the heart of the case study method (although multi-methods don't just apply to case studies). This is the notion of *convergence*: different kinds of evidence, gathered in different ways, but bearing on the same point.

- As the *main* technique when the primary purpose is explanatory description. Describing what you see and explaining it: what could be simpler than that? In fact this is one of the most difficult kinds of observation of all. Like informal interviewing it can seem natural and easy, but it is a sophisticated business. Being a good observer, like being a good witness, is not a normal, natural activity. It requires discipline and concentration – without which you won't 'see'. If we are dealing with individuals, *video* can be a great help because the same observation can be repeated many times: and each time you will see more. For example, if your case study involves mothers and their deaf babies it may only be by replaying video sequences several times that you see how they communicate with each other. Watching precisely what people do can be very illuminating. It can also help you to understand better what people are about: as we said earlier, particularly important if people can't express themselves in other ways. A good example of this which also shows the particular power of the precise description of what is observed is given in the following boxed quotation.

The researcher Sarah Hall was investigating the value of artists/designers working with hospital patients. In this instance, long-stay patients in a hospital for the elderly in Glasgow. It would be easy to write generalities to justify this sort of activity, although these might not be particularly convincing. Hall focused on *exactly* what happened when patients with sometimes severe medical conditions were exposed to this kind of opportunity.

The particular patient to be described was an elderly Asian woman who had suffered a stroke leaving her paralysed throughout the right side of her body. She was confined to a wheelchair and had completely lost the power of speech.

After examining the materials and observing the other patients' tentative beginnings, she chose a paintbrush and moved a palette of acrylic paints into position. Her first paintings were very basic and crude circular blobs of a single colour, apparently randomly spaced and covering the paper's surface. Joginder had difficulty holding the paintbrush in her left hand, clutching it firmly in an awkward clenched grip, which restricted the range of movements she was able to employ. Despite a water pot beside her, she made no attempt to dip the brush into the water before or after applying the paint to the brush and painted until the brush was dry before applying more paint. Other brushes in varying sizes were placed beside her, but once she had made her initial choice the others were ignored. Similarly with the paint selection: throughout the first few workshops Joginder continued to paint using only one brush and one colour per painting although she did vary the colour selection from one work to another.

It was a basic but very encouraging beginning as she

appeared to be totally engrossed when working and was visibly excited by the process as well as the results. She would only release the brush and stop painting once she had finished and was always eager to start again once a new piece of paper was selected. Although Joginder was unable to speak, and her understanding of English was reportedly limited, she definitely responded to encouraging comments and discussion concerning her work from the other patients.

The next stage of development

After several weeks of painting she began to take an interest in some of the other materials that were available. Although Joginder's paintings had developed considerably in a relatively short time, her abilities to control and manipulate a paintbrush appeared to be holding her back and she seemed to sense this. Having begun to realise her abilities and potential she was keen to experiment with another medium. Oil bars seemed a viable alternative to the acrylic paints and brushes she had begun with as these sticks of oil paint were relatively easy to handle and there were a multitude of colours to choose from. Joginder happily swapped the paint and brushes for the oil bars and it was immediately apparent that she was more adept and comfortable in using them. Initially she drew directly onto paper and then embarked on a series of monoprints by applying the oil bars onto glass, spraying a fine mist of turps onto the image and then printing it onto paper.

   The process is relatively simple yet the results can be spectacular and Joginder positively delighted in this. When offered paint and brushes again she flatly refused and reached out for the oil bars indignantly. It was strangely impressive that she had become so self-assured and assertive in such a relatively short time. (From: Hall (1996), in Gillham, Bill (ed.) *The Challenge of Age*, Glasgow: The Foulis Press, pp. 28–9.)

This account has been quoted at moderate length because it conveys the quality of careful observation and description and the power of the evidenced argument of which it forms a part. It is more convincing than generalizations and rhetoric.

Participant v. detached/structured observation

With the preceding example in mind we can get a fix on participant observation as against more structured techniques.

The following is an attempt to present the distinctions between these two approaches.

Participant	Detached
• Mainly descriptive/ interpretative, i.e. *qualitative*	• mainly analytic/categorical, i.e. *quantitative*
• subjective/humanistic	• objective
• emphasis on meaning/ interpretation	• emphasis on observed behaviour
• largely informal	• formal, disciplined
• flexible on information collection	• highly structured in data collection
• analysis primarily interpretative	• analysis primarily quantitative

From this it can be seen that detached observation is much more in the traditionally 'scientific' camp, i.e. the observable and measurable. Does that mean it is out of place in a case study? The answer has to be certainly not. Case study research (like a judicial inquiry) will make use of all available evidence. So if, for example, your research concerns playground bullying, apart from looking at school records of incidents, the systematic detailed observation of the *number* of incidents and *who* bullies *whom* might be an important part of your investigation. And such a systematic, structured approach may be indispensable when you have large numbers of children milling around.

Having made that simple oppositional comparison we can go on to look at the methods in more detail.

Participant observation: data collection

The first requirement for the participant observer is to identify himself or herself: who you are, where you're from, what you are trying to do or find out. The latter is particularly important. It won't *bias* the members of the group. You will only bias them if you say what answers or results you expect to find. Telling them your purpose is part of your openness, much of your identity, and it may be helpful. Information may be brought to you and members of the group may be encouraged to be more noticing and analytic of, for example, group processes or behaviour. This relates to the notion of *trust*. Helpfulness and disclosure from individuals or members of a group or institution – indispensable qualities – are going to depend on the building up of confidence in you as a person: that you are reasonable, straightforward, and sympathetic to their endeavours. The effects of this are most readily apparent in interviews (see chapter 8). People will disclose a great deal if they feel they trust you.

So you work on your relationship with the individual(s) concerned. But you have to be wary about forming (or appearing to form) relationships with particular members of a group (a caution we've expressed earlier): this may alienate you from the rest of the group.

You start with *descriptive* observation: the setting, the people, activities, events, *apparent* feelings. A general picture of what's on the surface.

Gradually (without losing sight of the overall picture) you focus in on, and seek out, those elements which are particularly related to your research aims. These you describe in

53

more detail, together with *provisional explanations* that seem to fit (the inductive method).

The maintenance of *field notes* is essential. We've referred to these on p. 24, but key points are worth reiterating and amplifying here. You include:

- running descriptions: your basic material;
- things you remembered later (your notebook should be always to hand);
- ideas and provisional explanations (their emergent character is a process not to be lost);
- personal impressions and feelings – even if you can't explain them: they may be the first hints of more important things;
- things to check up or find out about – star or highlight these so that you don't overlook them.

As mentioned earlier you 'write up' your rough notes – without tidying the content – promptly and regularly. This has the effect of running them through your mind again. It is also good practice to read through your recent notes before you next go on site: this will help you to focus and plan your time.

This is also a process where you should be challenging yourself. Am I going off course? Have I got the wrong end of the stick? Do my aims and research questions still stand? What do I need to be doing differently?

Structured observation: data collection

This is a technique to be used sparingly: it takes time in planning, is very time-consuming, and yields limited information. But this information can be highly specific on key points of evidence.

It is behavioural in the sense that you focus on specific

behaviours: and you need to be clear *exactly* what it is you are observing. For example:

- in a day nursery how long babies are left crying before someone attends to them;
- how many children are 'isolated' – on their own – in a school playground;
- how often workers on a shop floor disregard machine safety procedures;
- how long people have to wait in an Accident and Emergency department;
- how many people stop to look at a particular painting in a gallery.

Note that all these involve some kind of counting or measuring – of time in relation to behaviour; of particular behaviours.

Structured observation is about *sampling* these behaviours, and there are two main approaches to it. First, *interval* sampling: taking a look every so often – perhaps only for a moment (how many people are looking at this painting NOW? how many children are playing on their own NOW?). Second, *event* sampling: a form of continuous observation where you note how often or when things happen (the baby has started crying – how long before someone comes to comfort her? how often have workers fed material into the machine without putting up the hand guard? and so on).

You use interval sampling when the behaviours happen at high frequency so that continuous observation is unnecessary to achieve a representative picture. You can fix the intervals so that your samples are quite frequent (every five minutes counting the number of isolated children). If the frequency is moderate, e.g. people stopping to look at a picture in a gallery, you may do your count for a five-minute period every half-hour (which means you could target other pictures for the same period/interval) in between times.

If behaviours are very low frequency (e.g. how many disruptive incidents – however defined – in this class with this teacher?) then you should use 'event' sampling. Similarly if the events are causally related over time then you would observe all the time, recording the events as they occurred (patient reporting to reception in Accident and Emergency; patient called for medical attention).

There is considerable flexibility here and you can see that the interval/event distinctions can become blurred. Remember that the method is there to serve the purposes of the research. 'Method' is not some sacred cow to be worshipped regardless.

The essential point is that the picture that emerges should be *representative*: typical of the total reality. You need to get enough data from sufficient observations to be reasonably sure of that.

Two things you need to be organized on:

- a clear specification of what is to be observed (and a clear grasp of why it's important);
- a clear procedure for recording your observations.

Preparing an observation schedule

You don't sit down and write out an observation schedule right out of your head, any more than you just sit down and write out a questionnaire. By 'don't' is meant 'shouldn't' because, of course, people often do exactly that: with disastrous results which they richly deserve.

So that we're not talking in abstractions let us look at an actual schedule.

If you are involved in a project which aims to increase opportunities for social play in a primary school break-time, then observation of the numbers of children on their own would be one kind of evidence. A 'base-line' set of observations would be particularly useful. You could do this by counting the number of isolated children at five-minute intervals – perhaps three times on each occasion. So over a period of a week you would have five sets of observations. The actual schedule might look like this:

Date: 2.3.00   Observer: B.G.

Time: 10.40–11.00   Interval: 5 minutes

Observation	No. of children isolated, i.e. not in social play with others
1	̶H̶̶H̶ ̶H̶̶H̶ I
2	̶H̶̶H̶ I
3	̶H̶̶H̶ III

There are several steps in getting up to this point:

1. *Unstructured observation.* This may be when the need for structured, focused observation became apparent. You get a 'feel' of how it might be possible to observe in a more structured way.
2. *Specifying what is to be observed.* This is something you need to get precisely clear in your own mind. In the case of 'socially isolated' children how exactly would you define that? Distance from other children? No apparent communication or interaction? Both? It's not a matter of what is *correct* but of you being *consistent*. Observation recording is impossible if you have to do too much making your mind up on the spot.
3. *Finding a good vantage point.* Can you see all you need to see adequately? Too far? Too close? Visibility obscured in some way?
4. *Is the schedule workable?* Have you given yourself an impossible task? Intervals too frequent or not frequent enough? Too much to record at a time?

5. *Are the practicalities a problem?* Is timing easy? Would an electronic event recorder or counter be easier than a manual checking system?

The essence of all this is the need for *schedule development*. Practice and rehearsals are indispensable. You are going to have to concentrate hard so you don't want to be plagued by procedural distractions on the day: you need to be *fluent* and confident in your use of the schedule. Only practical try-outs will get you to that point.

8

Interviewing

As we have said earlier, this is an inadequate term for the range of ways in which you can get people to give you the information and insights you seek.

But this chapter itself is inadequate in a different way – in that it cannot give full coverage of its subject. Two parallel books in this series (*The Research Interview* and *Developing a Questionnaire*) deal comprehensively and in detail with what this chapter covers in about five thousand words. This can therefore only be a summary introduction and should be treated as such. It is sufficient to clarify the main kinds of interviewing and what they involve so that you can place them in relation to your particular research project. They are not sufficient at a level of practical and conceptual detail.

We reproduce first a table of the different dimensions of interviewing (Table 8.1), which appears elsewhere in the series.

'Listening in' and the occasional clarifying question is part of 'observation'. Questionnaires are at the most structured end of the continuum and are not usually used in case study research; but they can have a place at least in simple, factual information collection (see below).

Both questionnaires and research interviews are usually seen as part of the *survey* main method, but interviews of one kind or another are indispensable in case study research. The important point is not to be rigid about what you can or

Table 8.1 The verbal data dimension

Unstructured ◀————————————————————————————▶ Structured

Listening to other people's conversation; a kind of verbal observation	Using 'natural' conversation to ask research questions	'Open-ended' interviews; just a few key open questions, e.g. 'élite interviewing'	Semi-structured interviews, i.e. open and closed questions	Recording schedules: in effect, verbally administered questionnaires	Semi-structured questionnaires: multiple choice and open questions	Structured questionnaires: simple, specific, closed questions

cannot do in case studies. If one kind of evidence is relevant, or could be of value, then you include it.

Is interviewing appropriate or possible?

Interviewing, on any scale, is enormously time-consuming – although this is not true of some forms of highly structured interviewing ('recording schedules' as above – in effect verbally administered questionnaires: to be dealt with later).

The 'time cost' is a major factor in deciding what place interviewing should have in your study. If large numbers of people are involved, then, for the lone researcher in particular, interviewing all of them is out of the question. However, *some* interviews will almost certainly be worth their place provided you can identify a small number who are key or representative. If you are doing individual case studies then interviewing is practicable and probably essential.

What other reasons are there for not doing interviews? We can list these quite simply.

1. If most of the questions you want to ask are 'closed' – straightforward, factual. A brief questionnaire is appropriate here provided your respondents are literate and responsive to this kind of thing. If not you may have to use a recording schedule.
2. If the people you want to interview are widely dispersed. *Telephone interviewing* is a possible alternative, but accessibility can be a problem here (people are busy at work, may not want to be bothered at home). And keeping a telephone interview going is a skill all of its own.
3. If you want to preserve anonymity – although the value and importance of this is much over-rated.
4. If a 100 per cent response rate (or much less) is not necessary. The paradox is that although questionnaires

are less demanding than interviews, people are much less likely to respond to them – although you can improve on this (see *Developing a Questionnaire*).

5. If the material is not particularly subtle or sensitive. However, even apparently straightforward questionnaires can easily be 'misunderstood' – and you can't correct that; a great strength of interviews is that you can pick up these nuances which are often quite subtle.

The overwhelming strength of the face-to-face interview is the 'richness' of the communication that is possible. Questionnaire data in particular can appear (and usually are) thin, abstract and superficial. The richness comes at a price, of course. It isn't just the time you give to the interview itself, it is the time involved in transcription and analysis – a factor of about ten *at least* is involved here.

In summary you use interview techniques when:

1. Small numbers of people are involved.
2. They are accessible.
3. They are 'key' and you can't afford to lose any.
4. Your questions (or the most significant ones) are mainly 'open' and require an extended response with prompts and probes from you to clarify the answers.
5. If the material is sensitive in character so that trust is involved: people will disclose things in a face-to-face interview that they will *not* disclose in an anonymous questionnaire.

Preparing the ground for interviewing

Interviewing, even in its most unstructured, 'natural' form is not something you rush into. You have to get to know the setting and the people. You have to establish your credibility and earn people's trust.

You spend a lot of time looking, and listening to others,

before you ask questions. And your first questions should be of a naturally occurring kind – referring to the table on page 62, those you can bring into ordinary conversation, which can be a research tool of some importance.

Using naturally occurring conversation

As you get to know the setting, and focus your aims and research questions, you will begin to see what you have to find out, and what will best be answered by asking questions; and at a slightly later stage what will best be answered in an interview setting.

But you can ask questions systematically without setting up an interview.

If you are 'participant' in the setting you can decide on a small number of questions you want answers to – and ask one or two of them of people as the opportunity naturally arises. The people in the setting will know your purpose is one of research enquiry so they will expect you to ask questions (and find that acceptable once you've 'earned your place'). And because they're not being formally interviewed they may give particularly revealing answers. You won't be recording them – but you should write down their responses as soon as possible and as *verbatim* as possible. The research log again.

The 'élite' interview

The term 'élite' is out of favour because it has inegalitarian connotations. But the term is conventional in research interviewing. Élite interviewing is when you interview someone in a position of authority, or especially expert or authoritative, people who are capable of giving answers with insight and a comprehensive grasp of what it is you are researching. A hospital administrator, a head teacher, a safety officer, a social work director, or whatever. Interviews with such people are relatively unstructured, for a number of reasons, and have rather special characteristics.

1. They will know more about the topic and the setting than you do: to a large extent they can tell *you* what questions you should be asking, what you need to know.
2. By virtue of their authority and experience they will have their own structuring of their knowledge. They will not tamely submit to being interviewed where you direct a series of questions at them.
3. The best you can hope for is that you will raise *topics* that they will respond to.
4. Where they can be particularly informative is where (and what) documents or records are to be found; other people you should particularly speak to; what you can and cannot expect to be able to do.
5. They will expect to have some control over what you do, and will usually demand a level of accountability and reporting back. If you can accept that, they, in return, can be important 'facilitators'.

The élite interview is something you will usually report very fully in your write-up. This is partly because it is 'key' – of central importance *vis-à-vis* other elements of your pattern of evidence; partly because it will lead you in to different areas of investigation (a direction which has to be acknowledged); and partly because it won't be susceptible to content analysis according to a common framework as with other 'semi-structured' interviews (see below).

Of course, some elements of it will be more relevant or important than others, and editing and summarizing will be necessary, but there should also be fairly extensive direct quotation, particularly of those elements that you want to cross-reference to other kinds of evidence.

Sometimes you will develop a kind of 'consultative'

relationship with this individual and, in any case, a follow-up interview later in your investigation – when you have further points to raise – will be productive.

The semi-structured interview

This is the most important form of interviewing in case study research. Well done, it can be the richest single source of data.

Its apparent simplicity is deceptive. If you are able to see an experienced interviewer at work (live, or on video) it can seem almost 'natural': there is a pace, a fluency, a responsiveness that seems to have nothing of 'technique' about it. This very flexibility is what makes the semi-structured interview such a productive research tool; and the 'naturalness' rests on a clear structure, carefully developed and practised.

All skilled performance is deceptively simple, because the 'performer' has subsumed technique – is, in fact, hardly aware of it.

So you don't use an interview for your actual research purposes until you are confident in its use. But, even more important, you don't use it until you are clear about two things:

- what the key issues are in your research investigation;
- what will *best* be answered in a face-to-face interview.

The need for economy in interviewing

Even one interview generates a huge amount of work for the researcher. As a simple rule-of-thumb, a one-hour interview (assuming you've tape-recorded it – recommended) is ten hours of transcription and almost as many hours of analysis.

So you have to control the number of interviews and their

length: the latter is particularly important. With practice and careful preparation you can get a great deal out of an interview lasting no more than 30 minutes: but you need to be firmly, though unobtrusively, in control.

You need to prune your list of question topics to those that are really *essential* for your research project and which *cannot be answered satisfactorily in any other way*. The questions you ask will be *open*, i.e. where the answer is open. For example: 'What do you think about teaching in an open-plan school?' The kind of answers you get to that sort of question are up to the person you're interviewing and largely unpredictable. That's where the element of *discovery* comes in. You are asking the interviewee to tell *you*: and they may do so at some length, not all of it on the topic. Being able to move people on when they have said what is to the point is a key skill in interviewing ('That's very interesting. Another thing I wanted to ask you was . . .', and so on).

We'll return to interviewing technique a little later.

Interview preparation

This is no quick process. There are three main elements:

- practising interviewing *per se*;
- developing and focusing the interview topics and questions;
- rehearsing the actual research interview itself.

You can practise interviewing as part of developing the questions and format that you'll use in the actual research interview which you'll need to rehearse (or pilot) once you've got it into shape.

However, it's useful to practise interviewing 'off' your topic, and an example of this is given below. Before we go on to that we need to run over the main elements in organizing an interview. These are:

- identifying key topics (you may have more than one question for some of these);
- framing questions (around five to ten is about right);
- checking that these questions are genuinely *open*, i.e. that they let the interviewee determine the answer and don't indicate a preferred answer;
- deciding on *prompts*: things you may need to remind the interviewee about (e.g. 'what about financial support?');
- the use of *probes*: getting the interviewee to tell you more about a particular topic ('I'm not quite clear about that', etc.);
- *recording* the interview (taking *verbatim* notes stalls the whole thing and involves on-the-spot selection that may be doubtful; and writing up afterwards can also miss key elements);
- *keeping the thing moving*: which means having all the above working efficiently.

A 'practice' interview

If you are part of a research course it is of great value to practise on your fellow students. What follows on p. 70 is an interview outline used by the author with some of his postgraduate students. It is largely self-explanatory.

In your actual research interview the prompts will have been derived from other data and/or previous interviews, i.e. pilots for the real thing. You will know that certain elements have to come up. If a particular interviewee omits to mention one you simply 'prompt' them by saying 'what about ...?'. You're not leading them because you're not determining or indicating the answer. What you are doing is ensuring that all the interviews have comparable coverage: *this is of central importance when you reach the stage of content analysis*.

Prompts are important, but so also are probes. In the same

Explain that the purpose of the research is to achieve a better fit for the course to students' needs.

Key questions

	Prompts (if necessary)
1. How did you come to take this course?	motivation information research orientation
2. What were your expectations of it?	level academic character work load
3. What difficulties has it presented you with?	work load organization of time unfamiliarity of material
4. What do you think you are getting out of it?	personally conceptually career direction
5. What use do you think it is going to be to you?	research direction jobs/career development changed perceptions

Explain what you are going to do in the data analysis, e.g. content analysis and classification of main categories . . . informing course development.

way that an interviewee may omit to mention a particular topic, so they may mention something that is obviously important and then move on too quickly. 'Probing' is a key skill (the companion volume in this series *The Research Interview* devotes a chapter to it); there are many ways of doing it, it has to sound natural, and it can be highly motivating to the interviewee ('That's a point I hadn't thought of; tell me more!').

Probes also exemplify the point that there is a great deal more to interviewing than simply asking questions. The semi-structured interview is both *flexible* and, at the same time, standardized. Every interview is 'unique' and personal, and yet covers essentially the same ground.

The use of tape recorders is strongly recommended. Of course, you have to ask the permission of the interviewee – in advance if possible – and you need to know what to do if they refuse. They usually won't refuse if you *explain* why it is helpful/important. These are the key points:

1. It's impossible to get a complete account any other way – and you don't want to miss anything.
2. If you write things down during the interview, that distracts you from what the interviewee is saying and interrupts the flow – this can be of critical importance: interviewing requires great concentration.
3. If you write things down you have to be selective – and it is difficult to decide on the spot what is really important.
4. Writing down can inhibit the interviewee – they usually appear to forget about the tape recorder when they're in full flow.
5. If you tape-record you can listen to the interview several times: *and you can discern more each time*.

Tape recorders are simple enough to use but you need to be sure that you are entirely familiar with the model you're using: it is galling in the extreme to find you've pressed the pause button and half a key interview is lost. You also need to make sure that you have spare batteries and, above all, that the *sound recording quality is good enough*. There is a special kind of stress involved in trying to transcribe or analyse a badly recorded interview. This 'technical' side is just one dimension of what has to be practised.

In an interview you are, critically, the research instrument – a phrase we've used before but more generally. In an interview the fine detail of how you handle yourself is important. As part of your practice sessions with your peers you should arrange to be videotaped. Most people react with horror to the idea. It's a curiously emotional business, but you just have to steel yourself to it. In short you have to learn to look at yourself in a detached manner. You will get a lot of information which is not really accessible in any other way.

Watch the playback on your own: there's a special kind of ignominy in watching 'your' video as part of a group.

Briefly you need to look out for these points:

- How you come across visually – in particular what you are communicating non-verbally. Do you appear to be listening? Do you appear interested? Are you attending to the non-verbal signals from the interviewee?
- Do you probe and prompt appropriately?
- Do you explain the purpose and uses of the interview research adequately?
- Do you move the interview along at the right pace?
- Do you focus and direct the interviewee in a clear but unobtrusive manner, i.e. have you control?
- Do you close the interview in a socially acceptable way?

There is a lot here, and what is presented in this chapter on this important technique is a bare summary, but sufficient for you to appreciate the character and complexity of this kind of interviewing.

Transcription and content analysis

Carrying out the interview and recording it is one thing; transcribing and analysing it is quite another. Transcription should be carried out as soon as possible after the actual interview: your memory will help you in hearing what is on the tape.

You cannot analyse an interview just by listening to it, although you can get a feel and an impression, and certain parts will stand out. But transcription – writing it down – is terribly time-consuming. It is at this point that the importance of moving the interview briskly along becomes apparent.

You can't really study an interview's content except in written form. But *verbatim* transcription brings home to you that much of what people say is redundant or repetitive.

The essence of content analysis is identifying *substantive* statements – statements that really say something. One short cut is to play the tape and stop it when one of these statements come up. Even so you'll have to do a good deal of to-ing and fro-ing and what you will have written down is necessarily discontinuous. If you do this you should ask someone else to double-check by doing the same kind of stop-go analysis to see whether they identify essentially the same statements. You do something similar with a complete transcription – as a check on your judgements.

In summary, this is how to do a content analysis (but see Chapter 8 in *The Research Interview*).

1. Take each transcript in turn.
2. Go through each one highlighting substantive state-ments (those that really make a point). Ignore repeti-tions, digressions and other clearly irrelevant material.
3. Some statements will be similar but if you feel they add something mark them up.
4. Take a break. If you try to do transcripts one after

another your concentration will become dulled. Two a day, well spaced, is a maximum. But don't space them *too* much or you'll lose the categories that will be forming in your mind.

5. When you've been through all the transcripts go back to the first one and read them through again. Are there any statements you've failed to highlight? Have you high-lighted some that aren't really 'substantive'? It may be useful to ask someone else to go through a set of unmarked transcripts, highlighting what they see as 'substantive' statements as a check on your judgement. Make any changes necessary.

6. Now comes the difficult, intellectually creative stage. You go back to the beginning again (after an interval!) and, going through the highlighted statements, try to derive a set of categories for the responses to each question. Give these a simple heading ('Safety training procedures', 'Playground bullying', 'Written guidance on prescription use', and so on). At this point all you are trying to do is get a list of categories. You'll get a lot from the first transcript, more from the next, but progressively fewer as you work through them all – because indivi-duals will be making essentially similar points. Depend-ing on the number of categories you are deriving, you may find it easier to go from one transcript to another dealing with one question at a time.

7. You then look at your list of categories and ask yourself whether some of them could be combined or, alterna-tively, split up. As you are compiling the list you will sense that some of the headings you've noted down are not adequate or necessary. There is more work to be done here.

8. Go through the transcripts, with your list of categories beside you. Check each substantive (highlighted) state-ment against the category list to see if it has somewhere to go. Mark '?' to those statements you cannot readily

assign to any category. Modify the wording of the category headings (or revise them entirely) so that they fit the statements better or can include 'query' statements. It may be that you will need to add new categories. If there are a lot of 'query' statements then you should deal with them at a separate stage: too many of these may indicate that your list of category headings is inadequate *or* that you have a lot of 'unique' statements that necessarily resist classification: see below.

9. Enter your categories on an analysis grid like the one in Figure 8.1. If you have a large number of categories for each question, make up a grid/spreadsheet for each of them rather than for the transcripts as a whole. The category headings go along the top, the names or codes of the respondents down the side. If you make the analysis sheets A3 size (or even larger) you'll be able to enter in the cells what the respondents actually said, or part of it. This is very useful when you come to write up. Category headings, remember, are simply a way of classifying the kinds of statements people have made: they don't tell you much on their own.

10. Go through the transcripts, assigning each substantive statement (where possible) to a category. Statements you can't assign have to be dealt with separately: 'unclassifiable' but *not* unimportant. Sometimes just one individual makes a key point. Put the *number* of the category against the statement on the transcript: this tells you that you've entered it and where it's gone; if you can't classify a statement mark it 'u.c.' (unclassifiable). On the analysis grid you can either *tick* the relevant box (this person made a statement which fits this category) or *write in the actual statement* or do *both* on separate sheets: one for a *count* analysis (how many people said this kind of thing) and one for a *meaning* analysis. Sometimes a count analysis is all that is required, but tabulating the actual statements has a

	Categories					
Respondents	1	2	3	4	5	6
1						
2						
3						
4						
5						
6						
7						
8						
9						
10						
11						
12						

Figure 8.1   Analysis grid for content analysis.

lot to recommend it: it brings the summary category to life, conveys the range of responses that come under it, and provides material for the qualitative analysis write-up that comes later. And even if you do just tick the box you need to make a note of exemplar quotes for each category. These categories can have a bland, uniform quality and, in a sense, lose a lot of information: you need to be able to bring them to life.

11. With your interviews analysed in this fashion you have the material for the final analysis and write-up *in conjunction with* the other kinds of data you've collected. That final stage – preparing your research report – is dealt with in Chapter 11.

Practising content analysis

Set out as above, content analysis seems a task of daunting complexity. But if you start with something simple then the essential logic of the process becomes apparent.

An exercise the author uses with students is to get them to write down on one side of A4 paper the positive and negative features of their course (8–10 students being involved). These are then photocopied and each student gets a complete set, which they have to content analyse. Because the responses are written in summary form, and deal with only one topic, they make for an easy introduction. At the same time the amount of work involved brings home precisely what a full-scale analysis involves.

Writing up a content analysis

A good example of the content analysis and writing up of interview data is given in the 1995 report published by the Family Policy Studies Centre on single lone mothers. The authors, Louie Burghes and Mark Brown, provided a national background context derived from government statistics which paints a graphic picture, but they supplemented this with an interview study of 31 such mothers in an approximate 'quota' sample, i.e. an approximation to a national representation. How representative this was is open to question, but the inclusion here is because the report illustrates the writing up of a content analysis, a sample of which is given in the box below.

Experience of motherhood

Most of the single lone mothers said they had found parenthood difficult. There were, however, nuances to their experiences. Most notably, many also talked about their positive enjoyment of bringing up children, so that for most of them motherhood was neither 'all good' or 'all bad'.

'I think you get a lot of joy out of having a child but ... they are hard work.'

'... it's hard 'cause you haven't got anyone – although I've got close family ... you've got to take on the role of father as well.'

For some, high expectations of motherhood had mostly been fulfilled:

'I loved being pregnant. I thought it was brilliant ... had this feeling of being worthy of something and I just felt ... radiant all the time. And I was looking forward to having the baby ... I couldn't wait for this little thing to look after and love.'

But not so for others:

'I didn't realise it would feel like it did ... I was so tired ... I wasn't prepared ... I don't think anybody is.'

'... it always seemed easy when it was somebody else's and you could give it back ... I just thought it'd be the same.'

From L. Burghes and M. Brown, *Single Lone Mothers: Problems, Prospects and Policies* (1995), p. 50.

This excerpt makes clear why interviewing is a central technique in case study research (and an important supplementary technique in survey research).

But it needs to be emphasized again that what is given here is only an introduction and should not be treated as a comprehensive guide to practice. Aspects of interviewing which are dealt with here in a page or two are given a chapter each in the parallel volume *The Research Interview*. What follows is an even more summary review of other interviewing techniques.

Telephone interviewing

Telephone interviewing – at one level or another – has come to the fore in the past decade, largely because it offers some of the virtues of the face-to-face interview, e.g. its responsiveness and reflexivity, but without the cost (in time and money) of setting up individual meetings. It is widely used in market research, often 'cold', i.e. without preparation or the prior agreement of the interviewee. It is extremely difficult to do even moderately well, but it has emerged as a widely used research tool especially in the USA. The technique of 'random digit dialling' can even be used to get a probability (random) sample of respondents. However, 'cold-calling' in a culture where telephone selling is often seen as a contemporary nuisance, can be a punishing experience.

It works best in small-scale research either if you know the respondents and arrange a telephone interview at a time that suits them or if you telephone (or write) first to explain what the interview is about and arrange a convenient time for you to call for the interview. It is, of course, perfectly feasible to *record* telephone interviews, which enables you to focus on responding to the person you are interviewing (keeping it going is a particular difficulty).

Group interviewing

This is one source of information, particularly useful for getting an early orientation on your research topic – asking simple open questions and then noting the range and kind of responses you get. Issues of conflict or disagreement may alert you to hidden complexities.

Group dynamics, however, can be a powerful distorting force. If there are marked differences in status within the group then those who are 'high status' will either dominate proceedings or inhibit others. This information itself is, of course, of some value. But attention to *group composition* is important, e.g. are all people of more or less the same status?; are women or men in a minority? Even if one 'equalizes', some individuals will tend to dominate, though skilful 'chairing' on your part will control this to some extent. *Your* attention and interest given to 'minority' members of the group may act as a strong, encouraging signal.

The group dynamic's potential for conflict is, in a sense, one of its strengths in that it may bring out tensions and reveal groupings not apparent in an individual interview or the routine process of everyday.

Questionnaires and recording schedules

These are at the structured end of the verbal-information-getting continuum and usually have a minor place in case studies (if they are used at all). They are, however, central to the survey main method. Questionnaires are a much over-used research technique because they are assumed to be easy to construct. That is a fallacy (see *Developing a Questionnaire* in this series). What is true is that they are easy to construct badly.

Questionnaires are of little use if *meaning* and *understanding* are primary concerns – but they have their niche in case studies.

Questionnaires have to be filled in by the respondent without any assistance – which is why questionnaire *design* and *development* is so crucial.

Recording schedules are also questionnaires but are given face-to-face – the sort of thing used by the market researchers who haunt our main shopping streets.

Both have some value in case studies as a way of getting straightforward, fairly factual information. It may be that factual data on employees in available records is either incomplete or lacking in important respects (educational qualifications, previous employment experience, for example). These are factual matters most easily pulled in by a *very short* questionnaire. The trouble with questionnaires is that people often ignore them or don't complete them properly (even if they're 'simple' and 'obvious'). In other words, data quality or completeness suffers.

With a recording schedule you can pin people down. It can be time-consuming, but you get your data and you are able to deal with 'misunderstandings'. It can also give you a chance to gather some data on summary opinions and judgements from a wider sample than you could hope to involve in a semi-structured interview.

How useful they would be in any particular research project depends on the value of the extra data they would provide. It is not difficult to keep a recording schedule of, say, a dozen to twenty questions down to about ten minutes. Analysis is simpler because the structured presentation and the 'closed-questions' format mean that answers are standardized. Closed questions are those where there is only one answer or the choice of answers is given (Which of these newspapers do you read?) – the opposite of the open-question format of the semi-structured interview.

9

Quantitative Data in Case Study Research

Case study research does not equate qualitative (descriptive, interpretative) methods and data only. They are predominant, but quantitative data and its analysis can add to the overall picture. Providing they are not too complex, there is something distinctly clarifying about numbers. Seductively so in that they can carry an air of precision that is spurious. But statistics only lie to those who don't understand them.

Sources of quantitative data

We need to remember that there are two kinds of statistics:

- *descriptive*: ways of summarizing numerical data – averages, totals, ranges, etc.;
- *inferential*: techniques which allow you to draw inferences – the extent of correlations, the significance of differences between groups, the significance of changes following an intervention, and so on.

Both may have a place in a case study.

Records may provide the basic data for these kinds of analyses. One of the most useful is annual (or monthly or whatever) statistics showing rates and possibly trends over time. These kinds of data are often well-kept for legal/

administrative reasons. They include such things as absences, accidents and staff turnover. And they can be displayed in various ways. Over time a line graph is usually easiest to read (because it has a 'continuous' look to it). Whether they are relevant to your study depends on what questions you are asking, but you need to be alert to their possible use. Sometimes, of course, they are central. If you are evaluating a large school's attempt to reduce accidents to children on its premises you would need to study the statistics very carefully. The first step is to display the data so that you can take a good look at it.

Other questions could follow from this:

- is there a seasonal effect?
- is there a sex difference?
- is there an age difference?
- are there changes in the kinds or locations of accidents?
- is there a difference in trends for accidents that required medical attention from those that didn't? (Maybe there are more accidents but fewer serious ones.)

Once you start setting your data up in summary descriptive form you will easily see what kind of questions you could or should ask of it, the answers to which will *cross-refer* to other kinds of data you've accumulated – what teachers, children and parents have told you; changes in playground supervision; what you've observed in the playground; the introduction of personal safety education; changes in recording procedures, and so on. Anything that might be relevant to the pattern you see in the accident figures is going to help you to understand.

Abstracting data from statistical records over time is a particularly useful way of making sense of and evaluating what you've been told, and what documents and other records show.

If you are investigating safety in a school where there have been new initiatives, e.g. safety education for children, safety training for staff, it makes sense to ask whether there is any evidence that safety has improved: i.e. what inferences can you draw?

Pattern-matching and time series analysis

These terms are essentially the same, but 'pattern-matching' usually refers to a predictive approach to intervention, i.e. specifying a post-intervention pattern of results/incidents that would either show 'effects' or 'no effects'. But both techniques come down to a series of data for different intervals (usually annual) over a period of time and with enough data 'pre-intervention' to make claims for changes/improvements to be credible. For example, if you only had accident statistics for *one* year pre-intervention, and the post-intervention rates were much better, it might be that that one year was untypically bad and that the *pattern* for previous years had been no different from the 'improved' rates. If you've got data for four or five years prior, and the rates for several years later are lower, or in steady decline, then it is more reasonable to assume that there is some causal relationship.

Reality, however, is not always so simple. Statistics don't speak for themselves: they have to be explained or interpreted and sometimes the 'obvious' explanation is likely to be the wrong one. Look at the three graphs in Figure 9.1.

Graph (a) shows an apparent 'effects' pattern: accident rates have dropped dramatically following the implementation of the safety-training procedures. Graph (b) shows an apparent 'no effects' pattern: rates have stayed more or less the same. Graph (c) shows an apparent 'deterioration' pattern: rates have increased following the new procedures.

All of these patterns require interpretation. Are they

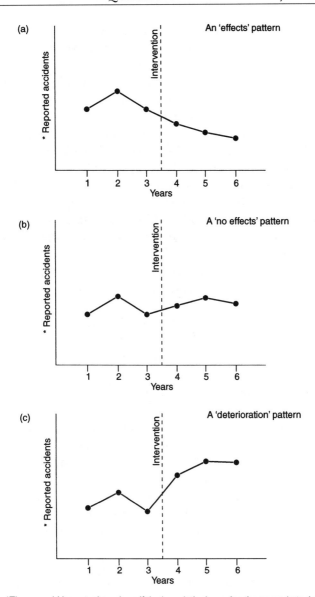

(a)   An 'effects' pattern

(b)   A 'no effects' pattern

(c)   A 'deterioration' pattern

*These could be actual numbers if the 'population' remains the same; 'rates' or percentages if it changes

Figure 9.1   Time series analysis.

actually saying what they appear to say? In each case you need to challenge the surface explanation. Maybe the true explanation is not the obvious one.

Graph (c) would appear to be the most baffling, so let us deal with that first. Going back to our raw data – the actual incidents that were recorded as accidents – we may find that, post-intervention, teachers have been recording many trivial accidents that would not usually have been recorded before. In other words the criteria for inclusion have changed. Interventions commonly have side-effects of this kind. It may be also that new legal requirements or professional procedures advised by unions have also had an effect (you may have picked these elements up from other sources).

If the data are re-analysed maintaining the same criteria for inclusion as operated earlier, the rates are shown to have declined.

It is not being asserted that this is always the case, but rather that you need to be alert to alternative, rather more complex explanations. If you are not, this is where statistics may lie.

The researcher needs to be rigorous in the search for alternative or supplementary explanations for *any* apparent consequence (or lack of it) in a time series analysis. It is rarely only the intervention that is new. This is where the multiple sources of evidence in a case study may help to provide a more valid picture.

Let us take graph (a): an apparent 'effects' pattern where accident rates have dropped steadily. Did anything else happen at the time of the safety education and training? Could that be more important as a 'cause'? Perhaps super-vision in the playground was increased? Perhaps play equip-ment was improved? Perhaps break-times were staggered so that the playground was less crowded? What do the people most directly involved think contributed to the improve-ment?

Graph (b) – the apparent 'no effects' pattern – presents another set of questions. Are we comparing like with like? The number of reported incidents remains the same and the criteria for inclusion haven't changed. However, perhaps when you sort accidents requiring medical attention from those that don't you find a marked decline in the former – masked by a modest increase in the latter; and perhaps here teachers are being more scrupulous in recording incidents 'on the margin' of concern.

Now these examples are hypothetical, but they illustrate the attitude of mind one has to bring to them.

Time series analysis can be used with successive observations (of the structured kind), usually where some changes are going to be introduced after a period of 'base-line' observations. But it may be that the technique is used simply to display 'normal' variations over time (times of day, days of the week, etc.).

Categorical analysis

Quantitative data in case studies quite often come in categories or can be put into them, usually to make comparisons between different groups (by age, gender, occupation, educational level, etc.).

For example:

- visits to the GP in the past six months (none or one or more) according to age or gender;
- employment or unemployment in school-leavers according to level of qualifications;
- negative or positive statements about computer use by age or gender.

You can put these into a 2 × 2 matrix: e.g.

	Visits to GP	**No visits**
M	8	20
F	15	7

Is there a significant difference here? By 'significant' is meant: how often could this apparent difference occur by chance? The statistic known as *chi square* enables you to put a precise 'probability' value on the answer to this question – a one in ten chance, or one in twenty, or whatever. If it could only have occurred, say, once in a hundred by chance, then it would be considered very significant. Being able to make this sort of statement can be used to complement the *qualitative* analysis of interview data, or simple questionnaire data. The calculation of chi square is described in a chapter in *Developing a Questionnaire*, or will be found in any standard statistical text.

Quantitative data has a special place in case study research in so far as it extends the range of evidence on the topics under investigation – and qualifies what we have learnt from other sources. This kind of cross-referencing is part of the *internal validity* of a case study: it all has to fit together – and theorizing (explanation) has to account for all of it.

Whatever kind of statistics we use (descriptive or inferential) the special rigour we have to bring to the outcome (using other evidence) is to ask: does it say what it appears to say? what might lie behind it? what other explanations are there?

In the 2 × 2 table above, which could be subjected to chi square, it *looks* as if there were a real difference between men and women and GP visits; is the difference 'significant'? Even if it is we need to ask: why? what lies behind it? In particular, are we comparing like with like? Are the circumstances of the men and women involved really similar?

For case study research operating in the real world, quantitative data analysis has to be subjected to the scrutiny of what it might *mean* – whether or not it is statistically significant. Even if the numbers involved don't yield a statistically significant difference, there may be important differences *in reality* and in more subtle human terms. Statistical significance is heavily dependent on the size of the numbers involved: if the numbers in the table on p. 89 were ten times bigger then differences would be much more likely to be 'significant'. But a qualitative analysis of the interviews with the individuals concerned would probably have demonstrated this in a different way.

10

Physical Artefacts

'Physical artefacts' is a rather clumsy term referring to anything that is *made*: and in variants of case studies this kind of evidence may be the most important of all. But even in case studies where this is not primary (and perhaps not even considered) it is a category to be conscious of. To the real-world researcher all evidence is of some potential value if it has a bearing on the aims of the project and the questions being asked.

There is an assumption that research evidence (and its presentation) has to be in *written* form. Apart from summary 'figures' of one kind or another, papers in research journals rarely include illustrations; they certainly don't include physical objects.

But even if you can't include them in your write-up, physical objects may be part of the database you have to maintain. And good quality photographs of these at least need to be included in your report.

Some kinds of evidence cannot be described or measured, only shown. There is an exact analogy here in the judicial process. In courts of law evidence is often of physical objects in considerable variety. More than that, judges will sometimes insist that jurors go to visit the physical setting of the crime as an aid to fuller understanding and better judgement.

Real-world researchers may find themselves in an exactly analogous position. How can they take the 'reader' of their report *there*? Skill in writing helps, but words are often not adequate: they can guide and can interpret but are often a poor substitute for the physical reality. Indeed there is a clue to their limitations here: that they can get in the way. Physical evidence has a direct quality: it is first-hand. You can read or listen to what others have to say about it but the actual thing is there for you to make up your own mind.

The visual dimension is uniquely powerful. In research it can bring your report to life – enable people to 'see' in the cognitive as well as the visual sense.

This is all very well but how can you get what may be large or bulky or heavy objects into a research report? Photographs, of good quality, are a minimum. But objects and materials can be stored (and their accessibility referred to). In some contexts (for example in art and design) an exhibition might be linked to the research report. You have to break out of the bounds of what is conventionally seen as a way of evidencing your research. The overriding question has to be: how adequate is the report to the range and quality of evidence that is relevant?

For example, in the chapter dealing with observation we talked about the value of video as a tool for observation analysis but also as a way of providing primary evidence for others to see the raw material of your descriptive analysis. Video can also be of value in presenting physical artefacts – it can move round them, 'look' at them from different angles, show them in use, and so on. Video is of special value when you are researching the process of making objects, where a static illustration cannot communicate – even with many successive illustrations – the activity of making and creating.

Physical artefacts as primary evidence

We've already talked about the 'primacy' of physical evidence in the appeal of its directness to our senses. But it is primary when the process of making is the essence of the research project. A burgeoning area of research is that concerned with the design process.

There are different kinds of design research (for example, of users trying out prototype products) but a fundamental one is to follow a designer through from first conception of a design idea to finished product. You end up with something attractive, novel and useful (we assume): it has a polished perfection. But a designer has to work through from first beginnings – at least, if it is a product of particular originality. How did they get there? The *process* has been largely neglected because it's the finished product that counts. But any understanding of design has to be rooted in what designers do. Moreover, if you are training designers, being able to give examples of the stages in the process (including, most importantly, the dead-ends and the things that go wrong) can be helpful, and encouraging to intending designers who lack confidence in achieving the sophisticated outcomes they see emerging from the workshops and offices of practising designers.

An influential use of case study process analysis is when the researcher researches *their own* creative activity. Such a researcher is in a privileged position: for one thing they're 'on hand' at all times. He or she also has privileged access to thoughts, insights, mental 'discoveries' which an external researcher could only achieve with difficulty – through interviewing, asking the designer to keep diaries, etc. It is equally valuable as a learning process, making young designers more reflective and more aware of what is involved.

Enabling the reader to 'see'

In the introduction to one of his books, Joseph Conrad wrote: 'My task is, by the power of the written word, to make you hear, to make you feel. It is, before all, to make you see. That – and no more. And it is everything.'

Conrad here meant 'see' in the sense of gaining insight into the motives and actions of his characters. And written language is uniquely powerful in that. But seeing in the visual sense gives you a different kind of insight.

For example, Sarah Hall's account of the developing artistic skill of an elderly stroke patient is quoted in the chapter on observation (pp. 52–3). This is a good example of a detailed account of what the writer had witnessed. But a fuller appreciation of what this elderly woman was about can only be achieved by seeing the works of art she produced. The exigencies of economic book production preclude illustrations in the text; but if you could see one of Joginder's wall-hangings you would read Hall's account with new eyes. You would see more, and understand better.

Most artefacts won't have quite that dramatic quality; nor will most cases have that kind of emotional appeal. But case studies quite often focus on exceptional groups or individuals.

Supposing, for example, your case study is of students with severe literacy difficulties in a secondary school. You can collate schools records; you can describe the setting; analyse the curriculum demands; you can interview the students themselves. But samples of work the students produced, unaided, would add to the reader's understanding, a better appreciation of the problems these students might have in coping with curriculum demands and the requirements of the employment market.

In the write-up of a case study (which is dealt with in the next chapter) these examples or illustrations are often consigned to an appendix, so that they don't interrupt the flow of the text. In quantity, and together, that makes sense. But they may be very much part of the narrative, even though they are not textual. Illustrations and samples are as much part of the chain of evidence as material that can be formed in words. They need to occur at the relevant point in the sequence because the text that follows will be read differently because of the sight of them.

The converse also applies: you don't include illustrations of artefacts just for the sake of it, to break up the text. The crucial test is (as for all evidence): what does it add? is the report richer for their inclusion? is the case understood differently or better? Which leads us into the next chapter.

11

The Research Report: Analysing and Presenting Your Findings

You will have been analysing and writing up your data as you proceed. This final stage, analysing the total array of data and presenting it adequately, is a formidable task. The more orderly you have been in your habits, the easier it will be. It isn't just that you will have made your material more accessible, but that your thinking will also have proceeded in an orderly fashion. You will have developed an overall grasp and understanding of the data 'in your head' – though this last stage will improve on that. Without this you will not be able to make sense of your material. It is not surprising that this is the point where people sometimes fail to realize the potential of what they've discovered.

There is no single way in which a research report can be made; and you are likely to use several of them. It can vary in length or emphasis, depending on its intended audience; it can be given live; it can be presented in conjunction with other work from various sources – as part of a large-scale survey or an exhibition, or a themed conference.

Having said that, there is usually a core report which includes everything of relevance, but even this has to be seen as something which presents a coherent, interpretive summary of what has been discovered, drawing together the essentials from the database of research evidence (much of which may have to go in appendices, the availability of the remainder being indicated).

Writing a case study research report is a demanding task because of:

- the variety of different kinds of evidence obtained in different ways;
- the skill required in weaving this evidence into a coherent narrative;
- the need to maintain the focus and direction determined by the overall aims and the specific research questions;
- the need to plot the successive revisions of the explanations or 'theories'.

The groundwork

It is here that the task of writing up is made more difficult by a lack of progressive organization in the collation of the research evidence and developments in the research design and theorizing. The task requires a grasp and degree of concentration which stretches one's capacity. As Yin (1989) rightly remarks, case study research, traditionally seen as 'soft', is extremely hard to do well; and that extends to the writing-up stage.

Your provisional, interim, summaries and your log book will be a great help at this stage. Essentially what you have to do is to review all the evidence, and your procedures. You will necessarily have developed an overall picture of what you've found and what it means. But parts of it will be hazy (and will largely remain so until you start writing). The weakness of this accumulated mental overview is that it will be selective and, in some respects, superficial.

You read your summaries, you carefully sift through the contents of your log book; and you review all of the evidence you have accumulated.

This detached, reflective overview is a key stage in the development of your study. In carrying it out you are not just reminding yourself of material that is partly forgotten, you are also making new discoveries in your understanding: you may have been partly conscious of these but the reviewing process brings them into sharp focus so that the whole pattern shifts – sometimes radically.

Research data analysis is an absorbing, demanding process requiring clear, undisturbed time. It helps to set out your different *kinds* of data in piles on a table. There is something about that simple device of external organization which helps your internal organization.

You move from one form of evidence to another, reading, studying and thinking. What you are looking for, in particular, are different *kinds* of evidence bearing on the same issues in your research. These multiple sources of evidence – which have to be related to each other – have to be woven into your narrative which itself represents what Yin calls a 'chain of evidence'. And alongside that chain of evidence comes your interpretation of it.

The structure of the research report

The structure of a traditional natural-sciences style journal paper follows a long-established format. A review of the literature from which issues that require further research are drawn; a clear specification of the research questions themselves; the methodology used to answer the questions; the results obtained; a discussion and analysis of these; the theoretical gains or developments appraised for their shortcomings; modification of theory suggested; the need for further research outlined. There is a beautiful logic to this deductive, hypothesis-testing model and it is easy to understand its intellectual appeal.

Hidden from view, however, is the less tidy, more intuitive, trial-and-error reality of intellectual discovery. The logic of the internal structure of a research paper does not usually reflect the untidy chronology of how it emerged. In a sense, part of the creative process, and meaning of the discovery is lost. Indeed, it is often only in the autobiographies of scientists that you learn how discoveries really take place. The scientific papers are not 'untrue', but they are not adequate as a representation of how knowledge is achieved.

The naturalistic researcher is more concerned to give an account of the reality of the research process. This has its own structure which has broad similarities to a traditional research report but has a quite different quality. How is this structure characterized? What are its essential components?

First, *chronology*: the order in which things happened. This is not quite the same as the *logic* of the research process: you will discover evidence that relates back to discoveries you made earlier; later insights will cause you to revise your understanding of what happened before. But in your write-up you can switch back and forth to link these up.

Second, *logical coherence*: chronology is not always going to be adequate as a way of presenting common themes or issues. You may need to bring these together and lay them side by side: especially important when you are cross-referring or transplanting different sources of data on the same issue.

Third, the *aim* of your research: which acts as a kind of retrospective effect on the structure. That's where you're going and that direction has to be kept in sight, whatever digressions may arise.

Fourth, your research *questions*: the development of these, in response to your increasingly clear grasp of the issues, is a continuous strand. These are the sub-plots of your narrative, the answers to which will (we hope) allow you to achieve your overall aim.

Fifth, your emergent *theorizing* or explanation of the issues you are dealing with. This is what gives meaning or *understanding* to what you are about. It is not enough to be descriptive, you have to be able to explain what you find. Why do boys truant more often than girls? Is academic failure a factor? If so, why does it affect some boys and not others? And so on. Theorizing drives your research questions, and both act to structure your narrative.

These structural elements of a naturalistic, case study report are a challenge to one's intellectual capacity: in particular to one's writing ability.

The business of writing

> Thought is not merely expressed in words; it comes into existence through them.
>
> Vygotsky, *Speech and Thought*

> Most of what we say and do is not necessary, and its omission would save both time and trouble. At every step, therefore, a man should ask himself, 'Is this one of the things that are superfluous?'.
>
> Marcus Aurelius, *Meditations*

Surprisingly little attention is given in research methods texts to the actual business of writing. There will be guidance on conventions and organization but almost nothing on how one writes or how this process interacts with one's thinking.

Good writing is not just a matter of having a style or avoiding jargon. Writing up a case study report is a skill of high order: a reduction to sufficiently detailed essentials for the reader to follow the reasoning-from-evidence process. This empirical stance (where evidence is primary and interpretation is firmly grounded in it) can result in an accessible account, where logic and meaning are transparent. This very transparency meets an essential requirement of research reporting; not just that one can follow the reasons and reasoning but that one can also see the limits: what could have been done differently and what should be done additionally.

And it isn't just the external reader that sees this, but also

97

the writer. When you are preparing to write, when you have reviewed your material, there comes a point where you have to make a start on getting it down on paper. There is a point of discomfort where you can't contain it in your head any longer. In a sense, your existing mental grasp is no longer adequate.

But when you do start to write, apart from easing the mental burden, freeing up mental space, so to speak, you discover an additional benefit. And that is that you are able to think about the products of your thinking. You will immediately perceive some inadequacies there; but you will also find that simply putting your thoughts into words acts back on your thinking to improve it.

This clarification process is perhaps the most important function of writing for the scholar. It harks back to the 'visibility' factor cited by Conrad and quoted earlier. Visual metaphors are commonly applied to good or bad writing: clarity, opacity, obscurity. Clear writing equates clear thinking, and that is what you have to work towards. It isn't just a matter of whether it reads well; fluent writing can have a glibness which means that you glide over the surface, engaging with nothing.

Words can run away with you. Good writing is clear writing where the reader can see your thinking, and that means stripping away non-essentials.

The specifics of writing

Writing a research report requires a disciplined momentum, and a high level of concentration. It is a process not to be interrupted, if at all possible: clear (mental) space is required. Here is a basic procedure:

1. Write a regular amount each day (1,000–1,500 words).
2. Read through the previous day's production before

starting again – this assists in the carryover, which will be going on, half-consciously, in between.

3. Write in the way where the actual mechanics of getting things down is least obtrusive – in longhand if your word-processing is not fluent.

4. At the weekend, assuming you've written longhand, word-process your week's output.

5. Go through this manually, improving the continuity and expression, making insertions where you feel you've missed something out.

6. Word-process your revision and print out a 'clean' hard copy.

7. Maintain this kind of discipline until you have a complete first draft.

8. *Then leave it alone for a fortnight* – put it out of your conscious mind as far as possible, i.e. dealing with the other things you've had to neglect.

9. This interval is to allow for the 'rotting down' process: giving the unconscious time to work.

10. When you return to your draft you will find that a lot of work has been going on. The need for alterations and additions will show up as 'obvious'. Having made these, prepare a new draft.

11. At this point give it to someone else to read and write comments on: not someone specialist in the topic you are writing on but someone who can appraise your writing and put detailed comments on your manuscript (most usefully: 'I don't understand this').

12. Getting your writing clearer shows up the deficiencies in your reasoning. It is at this point that 'specialist' feedback – perhaps from a supervisor – is appropriate: when your evidence and argument are clear enough for the inadequacies to be apparent.

By now you are almost there, although you will go on with fine-tuning for a while. However, this is mainly the stage where you check over the conventions (of referencing, spacing, sub-titling, etc.) that are required – and these vary as much as the positioning of controls on different makes of cars. You have to ascertain which model you are working to.

If you are prepared to work at your writing you can achieve a final result that will surprise you; writing is all about rewriting.

The Power of the Case Study

The meticulous description of a case can have an impact greater than almost any other form of research report.

This potency is reflected in the impact of single cases that are not research at all, but the subject of investigative journalism or judicial inquiries. The death of a vulnerable child may lead to major changes in legislation or the organization of care systems. These are general lessons drawn from a single incident. The case is unarguable: *it happened*, and something must be done.

In medicine, a single case concerning serious side-effects reported in a medical journal by a busy GP who has used a new drug with her patients, can throw into confusion the findings from elaborate and carefully controlled clinical trials. But single cases can carry a powerful argument even when they do not have this 'life or death' quality.

Widely held assumptions – in the public mind, as well as by academics – can be challenged in a similar way. In the 1950s an American psychologist reported the case of a young man with Down's syndrome whose tested IQ was 43 but whose mother had not accepted psychologists' and doctors' pronouncements on his capabilities, and who was found on re-assessment after her death to have a reading level at the 8th grade (14 year level) and maths level at the 6th grade (12 year level) – rather better than many intellectually 'normal' adults – as well as being competent in day-to-day tasks. This challenged the notion of 'IQ' as an index of capacity as well as assumptions about the general competence of people with 'low IQs'. Other single cases of this kind have altered our understanding of what IQ means: that it doesn't set a limit on what people can achieve.

Not all case studies can have this revelatory quality, something that challenges the existing order of things. Sometimes an insight into people's lives is what is required for better understanding and an improved response or attitude: a simple description of how an elderly person or a lone parent copes with their daily lives, for example.

Individuals or organizations, can both be 'illuminated' by case studies. A factory that is in decline, an inner-city school that is working back from a disadvantaged position: these institutions' direction and achievements or failures can be illuminated by a case study of the *process* of change, of decay or improvement. Case study research is a method not to be wasted on issues that are unimportant. Its real power is in part a function of the uses to which it is put.

Acknowledgements and Recommended Further Reading

It is important to acknowledge the author's intellectual indebtedness to the work of Robert K. Yin, whose book *Case Study Research: Design and Methods* (in various editions 1984, 1989, 1994), and published by Sage Publications, has done more than anything else to establish the case study as a legitimate mode of research.

A similar debt is due to the various works of Yvonna S. Lincoln and Egon G. Guba, whose key book is probably the 1985 *Naturalistic Inquiry*, also published by Sage Publications. It should be noted that their terminology and thinking have shifted somewhat since then.

Both books are *recommended further reading*.

Mrs Jane Cuthill produced the successive drafts of the manuscript with a speed and skill I have come to take for granted. My wife Judith polished the writing and corrected lapses of taste.

Postgraduate students at the University of Strathclyde and the Glasgow School of Art made demands that led me to clarify my thinking and not take too much for granted.

Index